KIDS COOKBOOK

THIS BOOK INCLUDES:
COOKING AND BAKING
A COOKBOOK FOR KIDS WHO LOVE TO COOK, BAKE AND EAT
100+ EASY, FUN AND HEALTHY RECIPES
TO MAKE WITH PARENTS AND SHARE WITH FRIENDS

Junior Health Institute

Copyright - 2020 - Junior Health Institute

All rights reserved.

The content contained within this book may not be reproduced, duplicated or transmitted without direct written permission from the author or the publisher.

Under no circumstances will any blame or legal responsibility be held against the publisher, or author, for any damages, reparation, or monetary loss due to the information contained within this book. Either directly or indirectly.

Legal Notice:

This book is copyright protected. This book is only for personal use. You cannot amend, distribute, sell, use, quote or paraphrase any part, or the content within this book, without the consent of the author or publisher.

Disclaimer Notice:

Please note the information contained within this document is for educational and entertainment purposes only. All effort has been executed to present accurate, up to date, and reliable, complete information. No warranties of any kind are declared or implied. Readers acknowledge that the author is not engaging in the rendering of legal, financial, medical or professional advice. The content within this book has been derived from various sources. Please consult a licensed professional before attempting any techniques outlined in this book.

By reading this document, the reader agrees that under no circumstances is the author responsible for any losses, direct or indirect, which are incurred as a result of the use of information contained within this document, including, but not limited to, - errors, omissions, or inaccuracies.

TABLE OF CONTENTS

FROM THE AUTHOR	6
GLOSSARY	8
NUTRITIONAL VALUES EXPLAINED	20
MOST COMMON INGREDIENTS	24
HOW TO MEASURE	28
PREPARING YOUR TABLE	30
INTRODUCTION TO "KID CHEF COOKING"	32
CHAPTER 1: CHEF'S TOOLS	34
CHAPTER 2: BREAKFAST RECIPES	36
CHAPTER 3: MAIN COURSE RECIPES	48
CHAPTER 4: SNACK RECIPES	60
CHAPTER 5: DESSERT RECIPES	72
CHAPTER 6: IDEAS FOR MORE COOKING FUN	84
CHAPTER 7: COOKING IDEAS TO DO TOGETHER	90
"KID CHEF COOKING" CONCLUSION	96
INTRODUCTION TO "KID CHEF BAKING"	98
CHAPTER 1: BAKER'S TOOLS	100
CHAPTER 2: BREAKFAST BAKING RECIPES	104
CHAPTER 3: MAIN COURSE BAKING RECIPES	116

TABLE OF CONTENTS

CHAPTER 4: BAKED SNACK RECIPES — 128

CHAPTER 5: BAKED DESSERT RECIPES — 140

CHAPTER 6: IDEAS FOR MORE BAKING FUN — 152

CHAPTER 7: BAKING IDEAS TO DO TOGETHER — 156

"KID CHEF BAKING" CONCLUSION — 158

EXTRA RECIPES — 160

BASIC NUTRITION AND WHY IT'S IMPORTANT (CHAPTER FOR PARENTS) — 182

BON APPETIT

COOK FOOD

FROM THE AUTHOR

COOKING AND BAKING ARE A GREAT CREATIVE OUTLET AND A GREAT WAY TO LET OFF STEAM

If you're learning how to cook and bake, you will find that working with the dough and pounding it out is a great way to let off the steam of a long school day or a long week. Stressed out thinking about report cards or that exam? Try beating up some pizza dough until you can make something amazingly delicious out of it!

LEARNING HOW TO COOK AND BAKE EXPANDS YOUR MIND AND HELPS YOU TO UNDERSTAND MORE ABOUT FLAVORS AND CUSTOMS OF THE WORLD AROUND YOU

Cooking and Baking new and wonderful things from all around the world can show you a lot about the flavors and customs that come from all over the world. Learning about new cultures and their customs helps us to be more connected as a human race, and allows us to be more open to other new experiences in the future.

COOKING AND BAKING YOUR OWN DELICIOUS ITEMS CAN SAVE YOU LOTS OF MONEY WHILE KEEPING YOUR HOME STOCKED WITH SOME OF THE MOST DELICIOUS FOODS THAT YOU'LL LOVE TO HAVE TIME AND TIME AGAIN!

Buying brownies, for instance, at the bakery can cost as much as $15 for a nice, big batch! When you make your own brownies at home, whether from a mix or scratch, you will be saving an average of about a dollar per brownie! With savings like that, it's a wonder anyone ever lets professionals do their baking for them, right? Well, if you get nice and experienced at making baked goods on your own, you can be the person that all your friends and family call when they're looking for the most delicious baked goods that anyone can make!

You can also bake for yourself and keep your favorite delicious treats on hand whenever you want them. Could you imagine having homemade chocolate chip cookies in the kitchen all the time because you made a batch, and they're still around for you to snack on? Jackpot!

YOU CAN SHARE YOUR FAVORITE THINGS WITH THE PEOPLE AROUND YOU AND COOKING WITH PEOPLE YOU CARE ABOUT IS ALWAYS A WONDERFUL BONDING EXPERIENCE

Cooking with the people that we know and love can be such a wonderful bonding experience. Learning together, rolling up your sleeves, talking about the recipe, getting to know more about how baking works and how each of the ingredients interacts with one another and working together to make something truly delicious is a wonderful way to spend time with someone that you care about. Consider finding a recipe that you and friends can follow the next time they come over to visit, once you've gained a little bit of cooking and baking skill of your own. Consider having an adult help you to roll out your own dough to make biscuits or croissants for the morning after an awesome sleepover with your pals!

EXPRESSING YOURSELF THROUGH COOKING AND BAKING IS A WONDERFUL WAY TO GO

When you start to learn more, and you start to remember how to make certain things on your own, you will find that you can express yourself and make your own wonderful creations in the kitchen. What an excellent feeling!

GLOSSARY

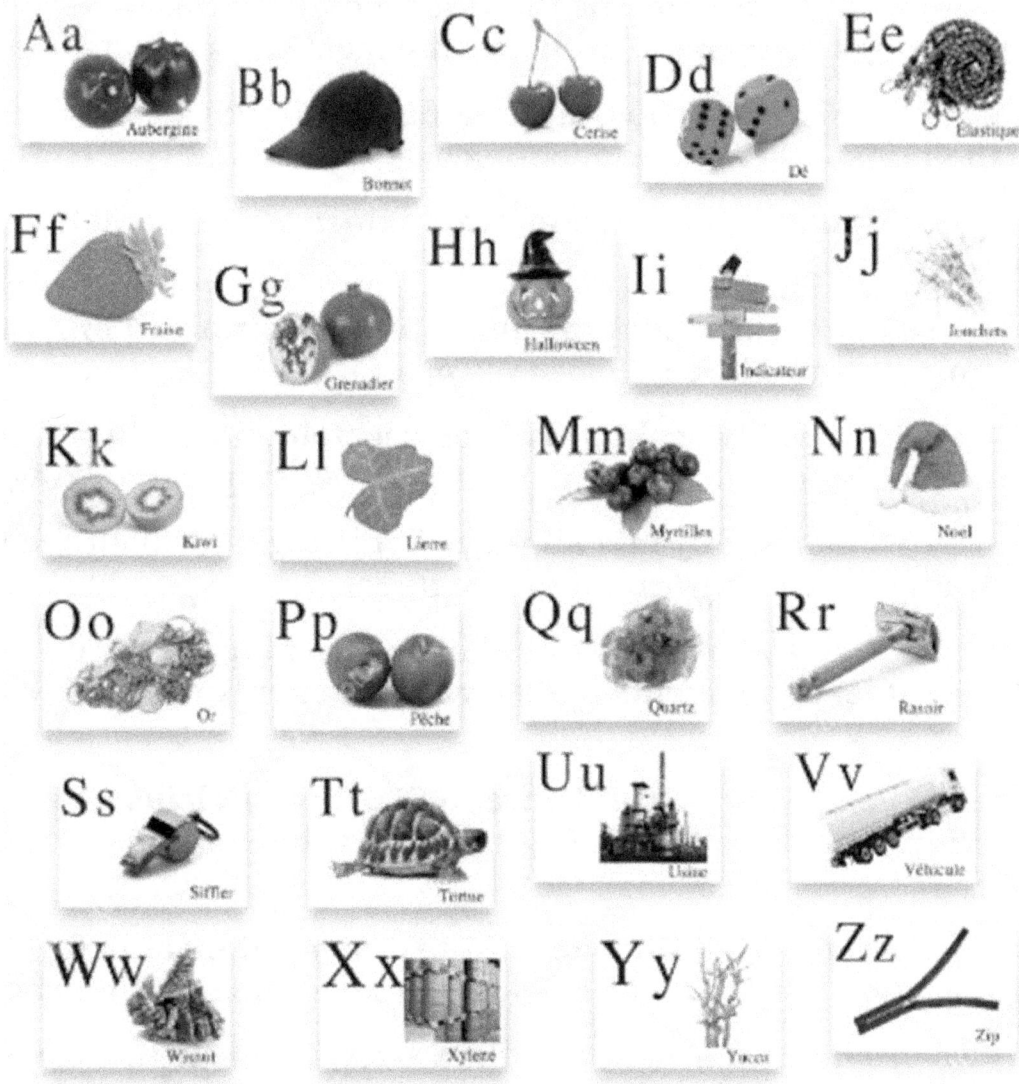

A

Acidulate (Verb) – **To add acid to something to brighten the flavors or to cut through the fatty properties of a dish.**

Al Dente (Adjective) – **When food (typically pasta) still has a slight firmness to it when bitten. This is achieved by cooking your pasta for slightly less time than usual.**

B

Bake (Verb) – To use an oven or enclosed and indirect heat source for cooking foods.

Barbecue (Verb) – To cook foods, typically meat over an open flame. This is usually done outdoors and can incorporate other elements like wood smoking.

Baste (Verb) – To shower a meat with either melted butter or its own juices periodically throughout cooking to ensure the meat stays moist over the heat.

Batter (Noun) – A mixture of flour and liquid that forms a coating for foods, which will then crisp when being deep-fried.

Batter (Verb) – To coat a piece of food in a mixture of flour and liquid before deep-frying.

Beat (Verb) – To use a whisk, fork, or mixer to work air into a mixture and to get the mixture evenly-colored.

Blanch (Verb) – To briefly scald a fruit or vegetable in boiling water, then remove it and plunge into an ice bath to immediately stop the cooking process.

Blend (Verb) – To thoroughly mix all ingredients together with the help of a blade to get things into a uniform, liquid texture.

Blind Bake (Noun) – The process of baking something, usually a pie crust, before the rest of its components to ensure all elements are done cooking at the same time.

Boil (Verb) – To heat water to 212° Fahrenheit or 100° Celcius, at which point bubbles form in the water, and it begins to turn to vapor. To cook food in boiling water.

Bone (Verb) – To remove all the bones from a piece of meat before cooking, typically done with a whole fish or chicken to make consumption easier.

Braise (Verb) – To lightly fry food and then strew it slowly in a closed pot or container.

Bread (Verb) – To coat food in breadcrumbs before cooking, to give it a crunchy, bready coating.

Broil (Verb) – To cook meat or fish in indirect heat, as in an oven, at a very high temperature so as to cook the food faster, and typically the food should be turned at least once during cooking.

Brown (Verb) – To cook meat (typically used in reference to ground meat) to change its pale or pink color to brown, indicating that it has been heated through and is now safe to eat.

C

Caramelize (Verb) – **To heat food during cooking, so it creates a pleasant, crisp, brown coating on the sides that touched the pan.**

Chop (Verb) – **To cut food into roughly bite-sized pieces using quick, heavy strokes with your knife. These cuts are typically somewhat inconsistent and less measured than others. If a recipe calls for items to be "finely chopped," it means that the pieces should be about half of bite-size. If a recipe calls for items to be "roughly chopped," it means the pieces should be slightly larger than bite-sized.**

Clarify (Verb) – **Typically with butter, to heat and remove impurities from a liquid by skimming them off the top or straining them. This can also be done when making your own broth or stock.**

Core (Verb) – **To remove the center section or core of a fruit. With an apple, this can be done with a vegetable peeler, an apple core, or it can be done with a knife if the person is highly skilled.**

Cream (Verb) – **The technique or softening a solid fat like butter or lard into a smooth mass, then blending it in with the other ingredients. This is most common in baking and can be done to make a smooth buttercream icing or a cookie dough.**

Crumb (noun) – **The pattern and size of the holes that form inside a cake or loaf that has been baked. For example, breads that are made with high-moisture dough are typically said to have an open and irregular crumb. Close-textured crumb comes for a drier dough.**

Cube (Verb) – **To cut into cubes. Typically your recipe will tell you how large the cubes should be, but one-inch cubes are typical.**

Cut In (Verb) – **To distribute a solid fat into your flour by using cutting motions with 2 knives in a scissor-like motion or by using a pastry blender until evenly divided into very tiny pieces.**

D

Dash (Noun) – **In many recipes, you will hear them call for "a dash of" an ingredient. Typically, a dash is roughly 1/16th of a teaspoon or 4-5 drops of a liquid; it's a very small amount that is just enough to add a hint of that flavor.**

Deep-Fry (Verb) – **Also known as "Deep fat frying," is a cooking method that calls for foods to be submerged into the hot oil. The oil should typically be heated to 375° Fahrenheit or 190° Celsius, but your recipe will often tell you if the oil will deviate from that. The fat used for this process can vary, but typical oils used are peanut oil, canola oil, vegetable oil, or lard.**

Deglaze (Verb) – **To heat a liquid, typically an acidic one like wine, to dissolve the browned, caramelized residue on the bottom of the pan to turn it into a sauce, soup, or gravy. This browned residue is known as "fond," which can also be found in this glossary.**

Degrease (Verb) – **To remove the fat or grease from the surface of a soup, sauce, stew, etc., you can use a spoon, bulb baster, strainer, or another helpful implement.**

Deseed (Verb) – **To take the seeds out of a fruit or vegetable.**

Devein (Verb) – **To remove the delicate black vein that runs along the back of a shrimp. Once the shell is removed or split along the back of the shrimp, this vein is revealed, and can simply be gently pried out with the tip of a paring knife and loosely pulled.**

Dice (Verb) – **To cut food into small cubes for even cooking. When dicing vegetables, it is important to dice all the pieces into a similar size. Your recipe will sometimes tell you how big your dices should be, but about ¾ of an inch is typical for the size of a dice.**

Dilute (Verb) – **To thin a liquid or mixture by adding more liquid to it, or to reduce the intensity of a flavor by adding liquid to it.**

Dissolve (Verb) – **To combine one ingredient with another to form a solution, as you would when you dissolve sugar in water.**

Dissolve (Verb) – **To melt or liquefy an ingredient, as you would with either** butter or chocolate.

Dollop (Noun) – A generous spoonful of a creamy or cohesive mixture that has been removed from the spoon with one firm flick of the wrist. One can also create the trademark round shape of a dollop by forming the mixture or cream.

Dot (Verb) – To place small bits or pieces of ingredients over, within, or around another ingredient, so as to achieve an even distribution of the first ingredient. For instance, you can dot pizza dough with cheese to ensure that the cheese melts evenly over the surface of the pie.

Dredge (Verb) – To coat wet or moistened foods with a dry ingredient before to cooking. For instance, a piece of chicken that has been marinating in buttermilk can be dredged through a mixture of flour, herbs, and spices before being made into fried chicken.

Dress (Verb) – To prepare food for cooking or serving so that it's pleasing to the eye, as you would dress a roasted turkey on holiday.

Dress (Verb) – To coat with a dressing or mixture in order to change or enhance the flavor, as you would with a salad.

Drippings (Noun) – The juices and fat remaining in the pan after the meat has been cooked. Drippings are commonly used in making sauces and gravies.

Drizzle (Verb) – To pour a very fine stream of a liquid, condiment, or syrup over a food in a decorative or pleasing pattern. This scatters the flavor all over the food, while also looking pleasing to the eye.

Dry-Fry (Verb) – to cook foods that are high in fat in a non-stick pan with no additional fat than what naturally comes from the meat that is being cooked.

Dust (Verb) – To lightly sprinkle a fine layer of powdered or granulated ingredients over. You can dust your French toast with powdered sugar for a little extra sweetness.

E

Emulsify (Verb) – To mix something completely together, so it becomes an emulsion.

Emulsion (Noun) – A liquid that is made of two or more liquids and other ingredients that have been completely mixed together to create a liquid of a new texture, as one would with oil and vinegar dressing.

F

Fillet (Noun) – A boneless piece of meat, poultry, or fish that is one thickness the whole way through.

Fillet (Verb) – To cut a piece of meat, so it is one uniform thickness the whole way through.

Flake (Verb) – To pull apart the natural seams of a protein, typically fish, so it can be combined with other ingredients.

Flambé (Verb) – To cook with a sprinkling of alcohol that allows the pan to burst into flames for several seconds, to add crust and flavor to the food in the pan.

Flute (Verb) – To make a decorative edge or pattern in pastry before it is baked, leaving the final product with a very pleasing and decorative design.

Fold (Verb) – A very precise term used for both cooking and baking, which calls for the careful combining of two ingredients or mixtures which have two different thicknesses or weights. This is accomplished by placing one ingredient on top of your mixture, pushing a large mixing spoon down to the bottom of the mixture, and lifting up, tucking the new ingredient into the mixture, thus keeping its texture and density more or less intact.

Fond (Noun) – From the French word for "base," the browned, caramelized residue left on the bottom of the pan after cooking meat and or vegetables, which can be deglazed and used for causes, soups, gravies, etc.

Fricassee (Noun) – A cooking method that combines both wet and dry heat. Fricassee falls between a sauté, in which no liquid is added, and a stew, which does contain liquids. Chicken fricassee is a traditional French dish that has a creamy white sauce.

Fry (Verb) – To cook food in hot oil or fat, whether by plunging the food into the fat or by cooking in a shallower pan of fat to get the desired crisp texture.

G

Garnish (Noun) – A decoration used to make your dish look more pleasing to the eye. You may have seen baked fish served with slices of lemon, or a cooked piece of chicken served over a bed of green lettuce. These bits are not meant to be eaten but are simply meant to be pleasing to the eye.

Garnish (Verb) – To add a decoration or embellishment to the plate as a way to please the eye of your diners.

Glaze (Noun) – A glossy coating that one can put on food, typically by pouring, dipping, dipping, or drizzling. Many glazes have flavors, some sweet, and some savory. Some glazes, like egg whites, are simply there to aid in keeping food looking glossy after their time in the oven.

Grate (Verb) – To shred an ingredient by dragging it over a grater or a rough surface meant to shred or break up food. Cheese and carrots can often be grated. Hash browns, before they are cooked, are grated potatoes.

Gratin (Noun) – A culinary technique that dictates an ingredient is topped with a browned crust, often using breadcrumbs, grated cheese, egg, or butter. Baked macaroni and cheese with a breadcrumb topping is a popular example of this.

Grease (Verb) – To rub down a pan or cooking dish with an oily or greasy substance such as non-stick spray, shortening, lard, butter, or oil, so the food that's in it doesn't get stuck to it during the baking process.

Grill (Verb) – To cook over a dry heat, typically direct heat, as one would on a grill outside. Grilling can happen indoors on a grill pan, but one misses the flavors, and unique caramelization one can get from direct heat. Grilling is almost always accompanied by linear markings on either side of the food that was grilled.

Grind (Verb) – To use a tool to crush something into smaller, more easily usable, or digestible pieces. One should grind peppercorns to make pepper, as it makes it much easier to eat and digest.

J

Julienne (Noun) – A style of cutting vegetables that leaves the pieces in very thin, square sticks.

K

Knead (Verb) – To mix a pliable dough by stretching, adding pressure, and rolling your palms into the dough. This forms gluten in the flour and makes it more pliable as you go.

Knock Back (Verb) – After a bread dough's first rise, to press it back down to burst the tiny air bubbles that have formed in the dough. This forces the bubbles to reform again in the shape and size that you want, which results in a smoother texture.

L

Lukewarm (Noun) – A temperature that is just slightly warmer than room temperature. It's not hot or particularly warm, but it's not cold, either.

M

Marinade (Noun) – A sauce that is usually made with things like spices, oil, vinegar, herbs, and items that will be used to soak raw meat before it is cooked and then eaten.

Marinate (Verb) – To allow a piece of meat or vegetables to sit in a flavorful sauce or liquid mixture to gain flavor for no less than 30 minutes, and up to 48 hours before cooking.

Mince (Verb) – To cut up or grind an ingredient into very small pieces. Typically, this word refers to meat, but it can be used for things such as garlic, which are meant to be used in very small pieces from time to time.

Mix (Verb) – To thoroughly combine ingredients together using a spoon to stir them all together.

P

Pan-broil (Verb) – To cook something, such as thin steaks fillets, or chops, in a pan on the stovetop, taking care to remove any fat that accumulates in the pan, such as with a turkey baster or a spoon.

Pan-fry (Verb) – To cook in a pan on the stovetop, using just enough fat or oil to keep the food from sticking and to form a tasty crust on either side of the food.

Pan-sear (Verb) – To cook in the pan at high temperature until a browned crust forms, before resuming cooking in another method such as baking, braising, grilling, sautéing, roasting, and more.

Parboil (Verb) – To cook food in boiling water until it's partially cooked. This is a way of cooking that uses no oil, which then allows you to add color and caramelization to the food for the remainder of the cooking process.

Pare (Verb) – To remove the skin of a fruit or vegetable using either a paring knife or vegetable peeler.

Peel (Verb) – To remove the skin of a fruit or vegetable using your hands, a paring knife, or a vegetable peeler as is needed.

Pickle (Verb) – To preserve by placing in a seasoned vinegar or brine mixture. Just about any food can be pickled!

Pinch (Noun) - In many recipes, you will hear them call for "a pinch of" an ingredient. Typically, a pinch is roughly 1/16th of a teaspoon or 4-5 drops of a liquid; it's a very small amount that is just enough to add a hint of that flavor.

Pit (Noun) – The hard center of a fruit like a peach, which must be removed before complete consumption of the fruit.

Pit (Noun) – A method of barbecue that calls for burying encased meat and vegetables under the surface of the earth and a source of heat.

Plank Cooking (Noun) – A method of cooking that calls for a plank of seasoned, flavorful wood (such as hickory) to be cooked underneath meat so that the meat can take on the flavors while being cooked in the oven by either baking or broiling.

Plump (Verb) – To rehydrate or to restore moisture to a food item that has been dehydrated.

Poach (Verb) – To submerge a food under a liquid, such as stock, broth, milk, or water for long enough to cook it. This is considered different from boiling or other wet methods of heating, as the temperature of the liquid is kept relatively low at about 160°-180° Fahrenheit, or 71°-82° Celsius.

Purée (Noun) – A smooth mixture of cooked food that has been blended, ground, pressed, or strained to be the consistency of a creamy paste.

Purée (Verb) – Blend, grind, press, or strain cooked food, so it takes on the consistency of a creamy paste.

R

Reduce (Verb) – To thicken a sauce or liquid mixture by simmering overheat until much of the liquid content evaporates.

Reduction (Noun) – A sauce that has been made using the process of reducing.

Refresh (Verb) – To submerge cooked food. Usually, this is done with vegetables, into an ice bath or under cold running water, to stop further cooking and to retain its vibrant color.

Render (Verb) – To slowly cook the fat out of a meat over low heat, and over a long period of time, so the fat becomes a liquid, rather than crisping up on the bottom of the pan. The fat that has been rendered can be used for other dishes.

Roast (Verb) – To cook using dry heat with no covering in temperatures starting at, at least or 300° Fahrenheit 150° Celsius. Cooking the food in an oven with no covering allows you to get a crispy layer on the outside of your dish, whereas coverings such as foil tend to keep moisture closed in on your dish.

S

Sauté (Verb) – **To cook food quickly in a minimal amount of oil or fat over higher heat.**

Scald (Verb) – **To heat milk over an indirect source and to heat the milk until just before it's boiling. When small bubbles form around the edges, you have reached the scalding point of milk.**

Scallop (Verb) – **To cook in Gratin style.**

Score (Verb) – **To make shallow cuts on the surface of your meat, fish, cakes, bread, etc., that can be decorative or which can aid in the cooking and absorption of flavor.**

Sear (Verb) – **To cook in the pan at a high temperature until a browned crust forms, before resuming cooking in another method such as baking, braising, grilling, sautéing, roasting, and more.**

Season (Verb) – **To add herbs, seasonings, juices, condiments, and spices to enhance and change its flavor or taste.**

Shallow Fry (Verb) – **To cook portion-sized cuts of food in a pan filled with one to two inches of oil. Foods are partially submitted into the hot oil and flipped halfway through to promote even cooking.**

Shred (Verb) – **To shred an ingredient by dragging it over a grater or a rough surface meant to shred or break up food. Or to use forks to pull apart cooked meat such as pork or chicken, so it's somewhat fibrous. Cheese and carrots can often be shredded. Hash browns, before they are cooked, are grated potatoes.**

Shuck (Verb) – **To remove the shell or outer casing of seafood or vegetables.**

Sift (Verb) – **To shake or grind a powder through a sieve or a strainer, so the powder has no lumps or large pieces in it.**

Simmer (Verb) – **To keep food on the heat, just below the boiling point to help flavors to develop and sauces to thicken.**

Skim (Verb) – **To use a spoon or other tool to pull congealed fat from the top of a soup, sauce or stew, or to remove impurities from a broth or stock as they're being pulled from the bones.**

Slice (Verb) – **To use a sharp knife to make thin, precise cuts, as one would do with a cucumber.**

Smidgen (Noun) – **In many recipes, you will hear them call for "a smidgen of" an ingredient. Typically, a pinch is roughly 1/16th of a teaspoon or 4-5 drops of a liquid; it's a very small amount that is just enough to add a hint of that flavor.**

Steam (Verb) — To expose food to hot steam, which brings the food to full cooked temperature. This can be done by placing a metal grate over boiling water and placing the food on the grate.

Steep (Verb) — To submerge dry ingredients like spices, herbs, coffee, and tea in hot water, and to leave them to soak for long enough for the flavors to extract from those ingredients.

Stew (Noun) — A thick, hearty soup that has been cooked for a long period of time, over low heat to develop flavors, and to reduce the moisture in the mixture.

Stew (Verb) — To slowly cook a mixture of liquid and solid ingredients over low heat for flavors to develop and for the liquid to thicken.

Stir (Verb) — To thoroughly combine ingredients all together using a spoon to mix them.

Stir-Fry (Noun) — A dish which is made of roughly chopped vegetables, meat, and soy sauce, which is lightly oiled and cooked all at once in a large pan such as a wok. Typically served over rice.

Stir-Fry (Verb) — To cook food in such a manner.

T

Toss (Verb) — To shake a bowl or pan, which contains both food and sauce, so as to thoroughly coat the food in the sauce.

W

Whip (Verb) — To vigorously mix an ingredient in such a way that incorporates air throughout it. Egg whites and heavy cream can be whipped into a much lighter, fluffier texture.

Whisk (Noun) — A cooking utensil, which has a network of stiff wires that allow air to be whipped into ingredients and to thoroughly mix things such as eggs into a cohesive texture.

Z

Zest (Noun) — The shredded rind of a citrus fruit.

Zest (Verb) — To shred the rind off of a citrus fruit.

NUTRITIONAL VALUES EXPLAINED

This chapter will cover something that you have no doubt seen on the packaging of some of your favorite foods! These are called Nutritional Facts labels, and they give you the total picture of all the different things that are in your foods, so you know if and when you're eating too much or just enough!

NUTRITION FACTS
8 SERVINGS PER CONTAINER SERVING SIZE 2/3 CUP (55G)
AMOUNT PER SERVING CALORIES 230
% DAILY VALUE *
TOTAL FAT 8G 10%
SATURATED FAT 1G
TRANS FAT 0G
CHOLESTEROL 0MG 0%
SODIUM 160MG 7%
TOTAL CARBOHYDRATE 37G 13%
DIETARY FIBER 4G
TOTAL SUGARS 12G
PROTEIN 3G 4%

VITAMIN D 2MCG 10%
CALCIUM 260MG 20%
IRON 8MG 45%
POTASSIUM 235M 6%

You want to make sure that your daily intake (how much you're eating) of each thing isn't too much and that you're getting all the right vitamins, fats, minerals, calories, proteins, and more. These labels help you to know all about what's really in your food, and how much you should be eating. For instance, did you know that some of your favorite crunchy, cheesy snacks are only supposed to be eaten by about a handful at a time? These labels tell you all kinds of things about the foods you're eating.

The facts on these labels often cover:

- How many servings are in the whole container (box, bag, etc.). A serving is how much of something you should be eating in one sitting
- How big a serving size is in cups, ounces, grams, etc.
- How many calories are in each serving
- How much of each nutrient such as protein and fat are in each serving
- How many vitamins and minerals are in each serving
- The percentage of your daily values that each of those numbers represents

Daily values are how much of each nutrient you're supposed to get in each day. So, if this label says that 8g of fat is 10% of your daily value, you can do a little bit of math to find that the total daily recommended value of fat is ten times that, or 80g. By looking at these nutritional facts labels, we can know more about what's in the foods we're eating, and it can help us to make sure that our bodies are getting all the things they should be getting, while not getting too much of the things that we should only have in small amounts.

Sodium is one of the things that you will want to monitor as you get older. Eating too much sodium from day to day can cause some problems in your body and can cause your health to drop in ways that aren't too pleasant. You don't want to feel less than your best because you're not eating all the right things, right? These labels can help us to stay within the recommended daily limits of these things, so we stay nice and healthy. Thanks to these labels, we can know all the things that are in the foods we're eating, we can make sure that we're not having too many of the bad things, we can have more of the good things, and we can feel great while we're doing it.

One of the things you've probably heard people talking about watching their carbohydrate intake. Carbohydrates come from starchy or sugary foods like potatoes and fruit, as well as things like chips and candy. Some people like to limit their carbohydrates to about 200 grams each day, while people who are very active and who have careers in sports or fitness will tend to have lots more because they need the energy.

Calories are one of the things that people will tend to count the most, which is why it's one of the biggest numbers on the Nutritional Facts label. It's recommended that people who are trying to maintain their weight (which means that they're not trying to lose or gain weight) take in about 2,000 calories each day. Doing this gives you enough energy to get through your day without getting groggy and tired, but doesn't give you so many calories that you start to put on weight. Your doctor can tell you just how many calories you should be eating each day in order to keep yourself feeling healthy and strong.

Let's do a little experiment involving the Nutritional Facts labels in your house! Go into your kitchen and see how many Nutritional Facts labels you can find in just five minutes. As you find them, take a look at them and see what's in each thing. Are any of the higher or lower in calories, fat, protein, and carbohydrates than you expected them to be? Take your notes here below!

MOST COMMON INGREDIENTS

As you get more and more comfortable with baking, you will realize more of the things that you like to use and the things that you need more than others. Each of the items in this chapter is not created equal, and some of them you may never need at all, but these are some kitchen basics that you should get familiar with if you're going to be baking or cooking more regularly.

Oils and Fats

Butter – Butter is a classic fat for cooking and for baking that has many, many purposes and a delicious flavor. Some people prefer to cut out butter, as it's high in fat and it might not be the healthiest fat to use when cooking. When it comes to baking, there are few substitutes that are as effective and delicious.

Olive Oil – Olive oil is a wonderful fat for multipurpose use and cooking. There are some breads (like focaccia) that require the hefty use of olive oil, and it's a great staple to have on hand.

Shortening – Shortening is used most commonly in baking and is a great fat to use for things like flaky biscuits, but you may or may not find that it works best for you. It's fairly inexpensive, and it lasts for a long time. There are even vegetable substitutes on the market if you're looking for something healthier.

Vegetable Oil – This is your essential, all-purpose oil. It's great for lubricating pans, frying, baking, and for recipes that call for a lot of oil because it's inexpensive and comes readily in large quantities. Canola oil is another oil that falls into this category, and it comes down to a matter of preference.

Vinegars

Balsamic Vinegar – This is a dark and robust vinegar that is good for salad dressings, sauces for chicken, and more. You might not find a lot of use for this in baking, but in recipes that call for it, it's hard to substitute it.

Red Wine Vinegar – This is a lighter vinegar that goes along well with flavors like Dijon and can be used in sauces and dressings. Neither of these vinegars can easily be substituted for the other.

Baking

Baking Powder – This is the founder of the white baking generations, and it is actually a mixture of baking soda, cream of tartar, and sometimes cornstarch. Be sure, when looking at your recipes, that you do not get this mixture confused with baking soda.

Baking Soda – Also known as bicarbonate of soda or sodium bicarbonate is the coarser of the white baking generations. This is usually used with a ratio of about ¼ tsp. to every cup of flour.

Brown Sugar – Brown sugar is stickier than white or granulated sugar, making it great for binding cookies. If you're looking to make softer, chewy cookies, brown sugar is something you'll want to have on hand!

Cake Flour – The protein content (gluten) in cake flour is slightly lower than all-purpose flour, resulting in a better texture for your cakes. If you like to make cakes and cupcakes from scratch, this is the flour you'll want to use!

Chocolate Chips – Having chocolate chips on hand at all times can be difficult if you're prone to snacking, but it's always good to have some on hand if you suddenly need to make some chocolate chip cookies, bread, or pancakes.

Cocoa Powder – This dark powder might not taste very good on its own (trust me, it doesn't), but with cocoa powder, sugar, and some other ingredients, brownies are just a few minutes away!

Corn Starch – This is mostly used for thickening, but it's a great product to have in your cabinet. It lasts for a long time, you don't need very much for each use, and it does its job very well.

Flour – You can use flour to make a wide variety of things from pancakes to batters and doughs, and you would do well to keep some on hand at all times. You just never know when you're going to need flour for a recipe, whether you're big into baking or not.

Powdered Sugar – Powdered sugar is one of those things that can't be substituted for another kind of sugar, no matter which way you slice it. If you have some powdered sugar on hand, you can always whip up some nice icing with nothing more than a little bit of milk and vanilla extract.

Sprinkles – Just like everything else in this baker's list, these can come in handy when you least expect it.

Sugar – Sugar can be used to even out the acidity or saltiness of a sauce or a dish and can be used in large part for baking as well. There are a lot of reasons one might need sugar, including for coffee and tea, so it's great to have on hand.

Vanilla Extract – Vanilla extract can be used for baking, but it can also be used to make complex and delicious flavors in other dishes that aren't even sweet!

There are no limits to the amazing things you can do in the kitchen.

Yeast – Yeast will make your bread rise, and you will likely need it unless you have self-rising flour. Yeast is a classic way to go, and it's inexpensive.

Seasonings

Chili Powder – This is actually a compound mixture that contains a lot of various things. Using chili powder, you can make things like your own chili, nachos and tacos, and some pretty delicious soups and stews.

Cinnamon – This is a classic that can be used on just about anything from your morning oatmeal to some delicious muffins. You can even use the cinnamon to help develop savory flavors and to give them just a hint of spice without the heat.

Cumin – If you've had Latin food and you know there's something specific in the flavors between all of them, but you don't quite know what it is. It's cumin. Cumin is the base for taco seasoning, and it's also used in a good deal of Asian cooking as well. You can always use this.

Curry Powder – You can buy store-bought curry powder, or you can make your own once you're a little more advanced in your cooking. Curry powder doesn't typically have the same ingredients in it when you buy from two different places. Generally, you'll find turmeric, coriander, cumin, and cinnamon in curry powders bought at common grocery stores, but you will find other things like fenugreek, mango powder, and cloves in other batches as well. Every household in India has a different mix for their curry powders, so you may need to sample a few and see what you like best!

Dried Basil – Perfect for giving sauces that classic Italian taste.

Dried Oregano – Perfect for making pizza and pasta sauces with that Italian flare you know and love.

Dried Parsley – A popular dried herb that brings a little bit of freshness to the dishes it's used in.

Dried Rosemary – This herb is perfect for poultry and, with a little bit of garlic and lemon, can make a heck of a flavor combination!

Dried Thyme – This herb is a bit earthier and can be used with poultry as well to help make the flavor more rounded.

Garlic Powder – Many home chefs will tell you that it doesn't matter what the dish calls for, they'll double the amount of garlic that's supposed to be in it. Garlic is a classic flavor that can bring life to your dishes.

Ground Black Pepper – This is a classic for any table and should be added to taste in every recipe you cook that isn't sweet.

Honey – Honey can add sweetness to sauces, it's great in tea, and it's ideal to have around the house when you need it.

Onion Powder – This is a great compliment to garlic powder, and it's good if you need a hint of a flavor of onions, but you don't want to cut up a whole onion for your dish. Perfect for seasoning chicken before a bake.

Paprika – There are several different kinds of paprika, but it's a great base to put in your seasoning mixes when you cook. By using paprika, you'll be sure there's a delicious, savory flavor in just about everything you make.

Salt – This is non-negotiable. You must salt your food appropriately, or it will not be good. Too little salt and the food is bland and boring. Too much salt, and it's almost painful to eat. Make sure you're tasting your food as you cook, so you know you're salting your food enough!

Canned and Dry Goods

Condensed Milk – This is used to moisten and thicken recipes while adding a creamy sweetness that doesn't involve too much moisture or work on your part. If a recipe called for sweetened condensed milk, there is little to no substitute.

Evaporated Milk – While being very similar to condensed milk, the major difference is sweetness. Condensed milk is sweetened, while evaporated milk is not.

Dried Fruits – Raisins, figs, apricots, and more are a great ingredient to put into your baked goods.

Nuts – Nuts are used as a great way to add a little bit of crunch to your brownies, a nice topping for croissants, and so much more. Baking without nuts is certainly possible, but you will encounter a lot of recipes containing nuts.

Cold Goods

Eggs – You will often find eggs as a wash or a binding agent in your baked goods, though it is possible to substitute if you prefer not to eat eggs or animal products.

Milk – Many recipes call for the use of milk as a moistener. If you prefer not to use milk with lactose or animal products at all, there are several nuts or soy alternatives that are great for baking. Lactose-free milk is another great option as well.

HOW TO MEASURE

In baking more than cooking, you must be familiar with and follow the exact measurements that are laid out in the recipes. Knowing what all the abbreviations for units of measurement will help you to be able to read your recipes and follow them exactly. One of the most classic blunders in cooking is needing 2 teaspoons of something and using 2 tablespoons instead, resulting in an over-salted or over-seasoned mess.

Teaspoon (tsp., t.)

A teaspoon is 1/3 of a tablespoon.

Tablespoon (tbsp., tb.)

A tablespoon is ½ of an ounce.

Gram (g.)

A gram is one-thousandth of a kilogram or about 1/28 of an ounce. This is generally used outside the US for measurements or for very small amounts of ingredients.

Ounce (oz.)

An ounce is 2 tablespoons or 28.3495 grams.

Cup (c.)

A cup is 8 ounces.

Pint (pt.)

A pint is two cups or 16 ounces.

Quart (qt.)

A quart is ¼ of a gallon or 32 ounces.

Gallon (gal.)

A gallon is four quarts or 128 ounces.

Pound (lb.)

A pound is 16 ounces.

You may find that you need to do some math when you're putting together the perfect recipe. If someone tells you that you need ¼ of a cup of something, but the packaging measures it in ounces, you want to make sure that you're getting enough of it, right? So you need to be able to tell that ¼ of a cup is ¼ of 8 ounces, which leaves you with what? 2 ounces. If you need 6 pints of something, but quarts are on sale at the grocery store, you might be able to save money by buying 3 quarts instead. Or, if a gallon is cheapest, you could just buy that and have a quart leftover for other recipes or other uses.

If you're trying to measure out one ounce of something and you've already used the teaspoon and don't want to dirty another dish, you can know that 6 teaspoons are one ounce since 3 teaspoons equal one tablespoon and 2 tablespoons equal 1 ounce. Once you get more familiar with measuring quantities of things, you will find it to be easier and easier.

Tip: How to Measure Using a Scale

Some materials and ingredients will need to be weighed with a scale, as those ingredients are measured by weight. Things like meat and flour can be weighed in order to tell you how much you're using or eating.

Many professional chefs prefer to weigh their flour rather than using cups and tablespoons to measure, as it gives you a more accurate picture of what you're adding to the recipe.

If you would like to weigh your ingredients in the kitchen, you will need a kitchen scale. Generally, these are fairly inexpensive and small scales. Digital ones are the easiest to balance and read, but there are certainly analog scales if that's what you prefer. To weigh your ingredients on a digital scale, you'll want to place your bowl or cup on the scale. Something with a wide mouth is best. Turn on the scale to set the tare weight. Tare weight is the weight of the things that are sitting on the scale, which you don't want factored into the final measurement. For instance, if you want to weigh a bowl of raw beans, you don't want the weight of the bowl in that figure. So you put the bowl on the scale first, turn it on and make sure the reading is at zero (there is usually a button to register a new tare weight just in case), and then pour the beans or other ingredients into the bowl for an accurate reading. If a recipe calls for one cup of flour, you want to weigh out 125g or 4.25 oz. It's crucial to make sure you measure out the right amounts of each ingredient, so nothing is out of proportion. You will find this is especially true of baking, whereas cooking can sometimes be a little looser on measurements.

PREPARING YOUR TABLE

When you're getting ready to bake, the first thing you want to do is make sure that your table, counter, or workspace is completely clear. You don't want to be moving things, washing dishes, and digging through the cabinets for the ingredients you need while you're in the middle of baking unless you have the downtime to do so.

Here's a little checklist that you can use to make sure that you've gotten all your tasks lined up in just the right way, so your baking process goes as smoothly as possible!

1. Have all the dishes that I will need to be washed and dried already?
2. Is the sink clear of dirty dishes, so I won't need to wash or move them while I'm trying to bake?
3. Have all my tools been cleaned, dried, and laid out for me to use?
4. Have all my ingredients been laid out so I can access them easily?
5. Do I have all the seasonings and condiments that I will need in order to make my creation delicious?
6. Have I set my oven to preheat at the right temperature?

Going down this checklist and making sure that you've gotten everything you need is a great way to save yourself a lot of time in the kitchen. There are few things worse than being at a critical stage when you need to add an ingredient, only to find that you don't have it laid out in front of you. This means that you need to run and find the ingredient, and hope that nothing got messed up when you were looking. In many cases, when you're baking, your hands will be covered with butter, flour, oil, or some other mess and you will need to pay your way through the cabinets with greasy fingers, or wash your hands and start all over again on your mixing once you've got the ingredients that you need.

Making sure that you have everything you need doesn't need to look like it does on cooking shows. You don't need a hundred little bowls with all your ingredients in them laid out before you, and you don't need to use every dish in the house just to bake. If this works for you and you prefer to do things this way that is perfectly fine.

One piece of advice that can help you if you're choosing to run your kitchen in this way is to wash dishes as you go. You will reach certain stages in the baking process when your dough needs to rest or when your creation is in the oven. When you're waiting for things like this, go ahead and rinse or wash your dishes and clean your sink out. You will find that if you decide not to do this, your kitchen will look like a whole bag of flour exploded in the middle of it and took every dish in the kitchen along with it. Taking five minutes while your creations are rising or baking can make a world of difference at the end of your labors when your creation is golden brown and delicious, and the kitchen is spotless in spite of all that went on in there.

Preparation is key when you're working in the kitchen, but so is leaving the kitchen the way you found it. If you don't own the home you're baking in; it can make your parents or the people who live in your home feel like they're being crowded with lots of dirty dishes. If you wash as you go, you won't feel like the dishes take very long at all!

CURIOSITY FOR PARENTS - THE MONTESSORI APPROACH

Setting the table is just one of the many activities that we all carry out every day. A job that can be done in a simple and fast way, as well as more slowly and accurately. The way we set can convey to others our desire for conviviality, the search for care, and beauty.

In short, setting the table is an activity that, in its simplicity, can talk about us and that can also represent a real means of development for the child. This had already been understood by Montessori. In fact, in the children's homes of the early twentieth century, it was planned that the children take turns preparing the table for their companions, serving the dishes to the diners and who, at the end of the meal, also took care of the arrangement of the whole.

But why is it important to offer the child the opportunity to carry out such activities? These are activities that allow the child to perform the actions that commonly take place in a living environment "for real," not simply by pretending. By properly preparing the environment, the child will thus have the opportunity to sweep, dust, decant, water, prepare food, comb, wash, dress and much, much more. And in carrying out these actions, he not only experiences the pleasure of acting as he sees the adults around him, but he puts all his skills and abilities into play, enriching his skills and progressing on an autonomous level. The child must know all the elements that he will use, know what their spatial arrangement on the table must be, be able to transport them, and handle them with agility and safety. Basically, this type of work is proposed around 30 months but is preceded by a series of preparatory activities for it.

The advice is to observe the child, his level of ability, and interests. This will make you understand the most suitable moment for the presentation of the activity and the degree of complexity to organize it.

INTRODUCTION TO "KID CHEF COOKING"

Congratulations on purchasing Kid Chef: Young Chef Cookbook - The Complete Cooking Book for Kids Who Love to Cook and Eat and thank you for doing so!

The following chapters will discuss everything you need to know about cooking so you can make delicious meals for your friends and family. These recipes are sure to impress and satisfy anyone who comes to your table. In these chapters, you will find all the information you will need to go from a beginner's understanding of cooking and how it works to an intermediate level that will allow you to prepare a large meal for everyone you love to enjoy! Whether you're looking to learn how to roast a whole chicken or make an egg without popping the yolk, this book can help you to get the information you need. The information in this book will fill you with confidence and allow you to try all sorts of new and delicious things.

CHAPTER 1: CHEF'S TOOLS

Baking Dishes – There are many dishes that you might want to cook in the oven. A ceramic dish that is deeper than your average cookie sheet or baking pan is the perfect tool for such a job and should be kept on hand if you like to make delicious meals for the whole family in the oven.

Blender – This might be one of the more seldom-used tools, but it's one of those things that you can't really come up with a replacement or substitute for when you're in a pinch and need one, so many chefs like to keep them on hand for when they need them. You can use a blender to even out the texture of a soup or a sauce, you can use it to make a base for something, and it's just the best tool for what it does.

Can Opener – Opening cans with a sticky or rusty can opener can slow down your whole rhythm when cooking, so it's best to get a can opener that can glide right through and open cans with ease.

Cutting Board – Don't cut your meat, fruit, and vegetables on the bare counter, or you'll scuff up the counters and dull your knives! Get a cutting board made of wood, resin, or plastic that will help keep your prep work safe and hygienic.

Food Processor – This might be one of the more seldom-used tools, but it's one of those things that you can't really come up with a replacement or substitute for when you're in a pinch and need one, so many chefs like to keep them on hand for when they need them. You can use a food processor to grind meat, make guacamole, chop up veggies into rough pieces, and so much more.

Grater – A classic cheese grater can be used for so many more things than just cheese. You can use grated things in many different recipes, so don't discount their use.

Hand Mixer – When you're putting together a thick mixture, a hand mixer can mean the difference between five minutes and thirty. When flour starts to bind with liquid and fat, it can get tough, or when potatoes need quick and smooth mashing, it can take a long time. A hand mixer cuts that work in half.

Kitchen Shears – These are large kitchen scissors that are very sharp. They are meant to cut through the thin backbones of chicken, the leaves of an artichoke, and so much more. Kitchen shears can make quick work of a lot of tasks.

Knives – Any chef will tell you that their knives are their most prized tools. A basic chef's knife is a good place to start, and you will find more knives with more uses as you gain experience and get better with them.

Pot – A large pot for cooking things like pasta and soup is essential in any kitchen. You just can't get by without one of these.

Saucepan – A medium saucepan will be called for in a large number of recipes that you'll find.

Skillet – Skillets are good for shallow-frying, sautéing, and more.

Slotted Spoon – This is a good tool to use when you want to pick up the solids in a pan without the liquid, or if you want to do a little bit of minor straining.

Spatula – Every chef needs a spatula! You can't even cook an egg without a spatula, so this is one of the very bare basics every chef needs.

Strainer – Whether you choose to go with a fine-mesh sieve or a colander, you will need a way to remove water or liquid from your dishes at some point or another. Colanders are typically used for draining pasta and sieves are used for rinsing rice before cooking, but both have many uses.

Thermometer – A meat thermometer or kitchen thermometer can tell you how far along your cooking is coming and how soon you will need to pull things off or out of the heat.

Timer – Most chefs will need a reminder when their time is up for things that are being cooked, especially if it's in the oven. Out of sight, out of mind, and you don't want your food in the oven to go out of mind!

Tongs – These are a precision tool that allows you to pick things up and flip or move them with ease. These can help you to do a lot of things and make the kitchen work a lot easier.

Vegetable Peeler – Whether you're peeling carrots, potatoes, apples, or something else, these make that work so much easier. Pros can use paring knives, but peelers are much more precise and faster.

Whisk – A whisk can sometimes be substituted for a fork, but a good whisk can help you whip up things that a fork generally can't. This tool is found at most chef's stations.

Wooden spoon – A wooden spoon is a classic tool that is a good one to use for sauces. It's soft enough that it won't scratch the bottoms of your pans (especially the non-stick pans) and it does a good job of getting things stirred.

Zester – You can't really zest with any other tool in your kitchen with the exception of the paring knife and the grater. A zester is far faster and easier to use, though so that is more highly recommended.

CHAPTER 2:
BREAKFAST RECIPES

DIFFICULT: BEGINNER   **SERVES: 4**

MEX SCRAMBLE

INGREDIENTS

- 8 eggs
- 1 can black beans
- 1 can diced tomatoes and green chiles
- 4 oz. shredded cheddar cheese
- Season as desired
- 1 tsp. cumin
- .5 tsp. chili powder
- 1 tsp. garlic powder
- 1 tsp. onion powder

DIRECTIONS

1. Drain and rinse beans and drain tomatoes and chiles.
2. Mix all seasonings together in a small bowl and set aside.
3. In a mixing bowl (large), beat eggs. Heat skillet over medium until hot.
4. Drizzle a little bit of olive oil into the pan to keep the eggs from sticking.
5. Pour eggs into the pan and stir gently with a spatula, adding seasonings, beans, tomatoes, and chiles while stirring. Stir until the eggs begin to firm.
6. Once eggs are cooked, top with cheese and serve!

Tools: *Can Opener, Mixing Bowl, Skillet, Spatula, Whisk*

DIFFICULT: BEGINNER **SERVES: 6**

HAM AND CHEESE MUFFIN

INGREDIENTS

- 12 eggs
- 6 oz. diced ham, cooked
- 6 oz. shredded cheddar cheese
- Season as desired
- 1 tsp. garlic powder
- 1 tsp. onion powder

DIRECTIONS

1. Ensure your oven is on and heated to 350°F or 180°C
2. In a mixing bowl (large), beat eggs and add seasoning.
3. Spray non-stick muffin pan with non-stick spray.
4. Pour eggs into the pan until they're about .75 of the way full.
5. Sprinkle ham and cheddar into the c and put pan into the oven.
6. Bake for 20 minutes or until a golden-brown crust forms.
7. Serve and enjoy!

Tools: *Measuring Spoons, Mixing Bowl, Muffin Tin, Non-Stick Spray, Skillet, Spatula, Whisk*

DIFFICULT: BEGINNER   SERVES: 6

CLASSIC BUTTERMILK PANCAKES

INGREDIENTS

- 4 T melted butter
- 2 c. buttermilk
- 2 lg. eggs
- .25 c. granulated sugar
- .5 tsp. salt
- 1 tsp. baking soda
- 2 tsp. baking powder
- 2 c. all-purpose flour

DIRECTIONS

1. In a mixing bowl (large), whisk flour, baking powder, baking soda, salt, and sugar together. In the center of the mixture, make a well and pour the eggs, buttermilk, and melted butter into it.
2. Whisk until thoroughly combined with some lumps.
3. Heat the skillet over medium heat and add butter or non-stick spray to prevent sticking.
4. Pour about .25 c of batter at a time into the heated pan and let sit until bubbles form and pop on the surface of the batter, about two minutes, then flip. Let cook for another 2 minutes or so before plating.
5. Serve with butter and your favorite pancake toppings!

Tools: *Measuring C, Measuring Spoons, Mixing Bowl, Skillet, Spatula, Whisk*

DIFFICULT: BEGINNER 　　　　　　　　　　　　　　　　　　　　　　**SERVES: 3**

FRENCH TOAST

INGREDIENTS

- 6 thick slices of bread
- 6 c. milk
- 2 eggs
- .25 tsp. ground cinnamon
- 1 tsp. vanilla extract
- .25 tsp. nutmeg
- Syrup
- Powdered Sugar

DIRECTIONS

1. In a large, shallow bowl, mix milk, eggs, seasonings, and vanilla. Whisk until thoroughly combined.
2. Heat the skillet over medium heat and add butter or non-stick spray to prevent sticking.
3. Once the pan is hot, place one slice of bread into the egg mixture and coat thoroughly. Gently lay into the pan and let cook until golden, then flip.
4. Repeat for each slice, then serve two slices per person.
5. Top with syrup or powdered sugar and enjoy!

Tools: *Measuring C, Measuring Spoons, Mixing Bowl, Skillet, Spatula, Whisk*

DIFFICULT: INTERMEDIATE **SERVES: 6-8**

FRENCH TOAST CASSEROLE

INGREDIENTS

- 5 lb. French or Italian bread ripped or cut into 1-inch pieces
- 1 c. pecans, coarsely chopped
- .6 c. packed light brown sugar
- .25 tsp. ground nutmeg
- .25 tsp. ground cinnamon
- 1 tsp. vanilla extract
- .5 T granulated sugar
- .75 c. heavy cream
- 1 c. whole milk
- 4 lg. eggs
- 4 T unsalted butter, softened

DIRECTIONS

1. Ensure your oven is on and heated to 350°F or 180°C.
2. In a mixing bowl (large), mix eggs, cream, milk, granulated sugar, vanilla, nutmeg, and cinnamon together until creamy and smooth. Pour mixture over bread.
3. Stir butter and brown sugar together until smooth, then add pecans.
4. Sprinkle butter-nut mixture over the bread and bake for about 1 hour until the top has taken on a golden quality brown.
5. Let stand for 10 minutes, then serve!

Tools: *Baking Dish, Mixing Bowl, Spatula, Whisk, Wooden Spoon*

DIFFICULT: BEGINNER **SERVES: 6**

SHAKSHUKA

INGREDIENTS

- 1 med. red bell pepper, seeded and diced
- 4 cloves garlic, minced
- 1 sm. bunch cilantro, finely chopped
- 1 sm. bunch parsley, finely chopped
- 1 med. onion, diced
- 6 lg. eggs
- 1 can (28 oz.) whole peeled tomatoes
- Season as desired
- 2 tsp. paprika
- 1 tsp. cumin
- .25 tsp. chili powder

DIRECTIONS

1. In a large pan over medium heat, add chopped bell pepper and onion. Cook until translucent and fragrant.
2. Add garlic and spices to the pan and stir thoroughly with a wooden spoon before allowing to cook for an additional minute.
3. Without draining the tomatoes, pour the can into the large pan and stir to incorporate. With your wooden spoon, break down the tomatoes into smaller, bite-sized chunks.
4. Using the serving spoon, make 6 wells in the stew, well away from one another. Break the eggs into the wells and cover. Let cook for 5-8 minutes or until the eggs are cooked.
5. Garnish with parsley and cilantro and serve!

Tools: *Can Opener, Chef's Knife, Cutting Board, Serving Spoon, Skillet, Spatula, Whisk, Wooden Spoon*

DIFFICULT: BEGINNER   SERVES: 4

BREAKFAST SCRAMBLE

INGREDIENTS

- 8 eggs
- 1 lb. breakfast sausage
- .5 med. diced onion
- 4 oz. shredded cheddar cheese
- Season as desired
- .5 tsp. dried parsley
- .5 tsp. paprika
- 1 tsp. garlic powder
- 1 tsp. onion powder

DIRECTIONS

1. Heat the skillet over medium heat with butter or non-stick spray to prevent sticking.
2. Brown sausage over medium, breaking it up with your spatula so it's in small, even pieces.
3. Once the meat is mostly browned, add diced onion to the pan and let cook until it's translucent.
4. In a large bowl, mix eggs, herbs, and spices until totally mixed.
5. Toss cheese into the pan and stir to incorporate fully.
6. Pour eggs into the pan over the sausage and use the spatula to continuously stir until fully cooked.
7. Serve!

Tools: *Chef's knife, Mixing Bowl, Skillet, Spatula, Whisk*

DIFFICULT: BEGINNER   **SERVES: 12**

BLUEBERRY OATMEAL MUFFINS

INGREDIENTS

- 1.25 c. instant oatmeal
- 1/3 c. granulated sugar
- 5 tsp. salt
- 1 c. all-purpose flour
- 1 c. milk
- 1 T baking powder
- .25 c. vegetable oil
- 1 egg
- 1 c. blueberries, rinsed and drained

DIRECTIONS

1. Ensure your oven is on and heated to 425°F of 220°C.
2. Combine all ingredients into a mixing bowl (large) before mixing well.
3. Spray a muffin tin with non-stick spray and fill each muffin tin about .6 of the way.
4. Bake for 20-25 minutes until the top has taken on a golden quality.
5. Serve!

Tools: *Mixing Bowl, Muffin Tin, Rubber Spatula, Whisk*

DIFFICULT: BEGINNER   **SERVES: 8**

FRUIT SALAD

INGREDIENTS

- 2 c. grapes
- 1 mango, chopped
- 2 apples, peeled and chopped
- 1 orange, wedges cut in half
- 3 kiwis, sliced
- 6 oz. raspberries
- 6 oz. blueberries
- 1 lb. strawberries, sliced

DIRECTIONS

1. Combine all ingredients into a mixing bowl (large) and cover.
2. Chill for 30 minutes and serve!

Tools: *Cutting Board, Paring Knife, Mixing Bowl*

DIFFICULT: BEGINNER **SERVES: 1**

CLASSIC OMELET

INGREDIENTS

- 2 eggs
- 1 T milk or water
- 2 oz. cheddar cheese
- Season as desired
- Garlic (1 pinch) powder
- A pinch of onion powder

DIRECTIONS

1. In a small bowl, combine seasonings, milk, and eggs and whisk until smooth.
2. Heat a skillet over medium heat and add butter or non-stick spray to prevent sticking.
3. Pour eggs into the pan and leave on the heat for 1-2 minutes until it begins to firm.
4. Sprinkle cheese onto one side of the omelet and slide the spatula under the other half to release it from the pan. Gently fold over and allow the cheese to melt.
5. Serve!

Tip: You can fill your omelet with just about anything you'd like, so don't be afraid to get creative!

Tools: *Skillet, Small Mixing Bowl, Spatula, Whisk*

CHAPTER 3:
MAIN COURSE RECIPES

DIFFICULT: BEGINNER   **SERVES: 8**

SPAGHETTI WITH MEAT SAUCE

INGREDIENTS

- 5 tsp. black pepper
- 1 can (16 oz.) tomato sauce
- 1 can (28 oz.) diced tomatoes
- 1 lb. ground beef
- 1 med. onion, diced
- 1 tsp. salt
- 16 oz. spaghetti noodles
- 2 tsp. dried basil
- 2 tsp. dried oregano
- 4 cloves garlic, minced

DIRECTIONS

1. In a large saucepan, brown the beef and top with all seasonings, mixing thoroughly.
2. Fill a large pot about .75 of the way with water, place over high heat, and drizzle a little olive oil into the water, as well as a heaping portion of salt. Stir to combine. Bring to a boil, then add pasta, stirring occasionally.
3. Add tomatoes and sauce to the pan and stir thoroughly to combine. Reduce heat to a simmer.
4. Strain pasta and serve, topping with sauce and parmesan cheese, if desired.

Tools: *Can Opener, Large Pot, Large Saucepan, Spatula, Wooden Spoon*

DIFFICULT: BEGINNER　　　　　　　　　　**SERVES: 4**

SMOTHERED CHICKEN BREASTS

INGREDIENTS

- 1 lb. chicken breasts
- 4 bacon slices
- 5 c shredded Colby-Monterey Jack cheese
- Garlic (1 pinch) powder for each breast
- A pinch of onion powder for each breast
- A pinch of rosemary for each breast

DIRECTIONS

1. Ensure your oven is on and heated to 425°F or 220°C.
2. Heat a skillet over medium and cook bacon until crisp.
3. Sprinkle seasonings over each breast and lay them into the pan. Heat about 5-6 minutes on each side until golden brown.
4. Lay chicken breasts on a cookie sheet and top with bacon and cheese. Cook at 425°F or 220°C for 10 minutes or until an internal temperature of 165°F or 75°C is reached.
5. Serve!

Tools: *Baking dish, Skillet*

DIFFICULT: BEGINNER   **SERVES: 6**

CHILI

INGREDIENTS

- 1 lb. ground beef
- 1 can (15 oz.) diced tomatoes
- 1 can (15 oz.) kidney beans
- 1 can (15 oz.) corn
- 4 tsp. chili powder
- 1 T onion powder
- 1 T garlic powder
- 2 tsp. cumin
- 2 tsp. dried parsley
- 2 tsp. salt
- .5 tsp. pepper

DIRECTIONS

1. Heat a large pot over medium and add butter or oil to prevent sticking.
2. Put beef in the pot to brown it and combine all seasonings into a small bowl before mixing well.
3. Sprinkle half of the seasoning mix over the beef and stir completely.
4. Strain and rinse corn and beans, then add to pot with tomatoes. Add remaining seasonings and stir to combine.
5. Cover and heat for 10 more minutes, or reduce heat and let simmer for up to 30 minutes.
6. Serve!

Tools: *Can Opener, Measuring Spoons, Pot, Wooden Spoon*

DIFFICULT: BEGINNER **SERVES: 4**

TACOS

INGREDIENTS

- 8 tortillas or crunchy taco shells
- 1 lb. ground beef
- 25 tsp. dried oregano
- 5 tsp. paprika
- 1 T chili powder
- 1 tsp. black pepper
- 1 tsp. garlic powder
- 1 tsp. onion powder
- 1 tsp. salt

DIRECTIONS

1. Heat a skillet over medium heat.
2. In a small bowl, combine all seasonings before mixing well.
3. Brown beef over medium heat and top with the seasoning mix, stirring thoroughly.
4. Add to taco shells and serve!

Tip: Add things like shredded lettuce, diced tomatoes, cheddar cheese, and sour cream if you'd like!

Tools: *Measuring Spoons, Skillet, Wooden Spoons*

DIFFICULT: BEGINNER   **SERVES: 4**

CHICKEN CAESAR SALAD

INGREDIENTS

- 1 lb. chicken breasts
- Shredded parmesan cheese
- 4-6 c. chopped romaine lettuce
- .5 c. Caesar dressing
- .5 c. garlic croutons
- Season as desired

DIRECTIONS

1. Warm a skillet over medium heat and season chicken breasts.
2. Cook the breasts over medium heat for 6-8 minutes until an internal temperature of 165°F or 75°C is reached.
3. In a large bowl, combine lettuce, chicken, cheese, and dressing. Toss with wooden spoon to mix thoroughly.
4. Serve!

Tools: *Mixing Bowl, Skillet, Wooden Spoon*

DIFFICULT: BEGINNER   **SERVES: 4**

MINESTRONE SOUP

INGREDIENTS

- 25 c. celery, chopped
- 5 c carrots, chopped
- 5 c. shredded cabbage
- 5 c. shredded parmesan cheese
- 5 tsp. pepper
- 1 (15 oz.) can stewed tomatoes
- 1.5 c. potatoes, cubed
- 1 can (15 oz.) cannellini beans
- 1 med. onion, chopped
- 1 qt. chicken broth
- 1 T tomato paste
- 1 tsp. salt
- 2 T dried parsley
- 4 oz. elbow macaroni
- 4 T butter

DIRECTIONS

1. Heat large pot over medium heat and melt butter.
2. Add onion, carrots, and celery and sauté for a few minutes.
3. Add beans, cabbage, parsley, tomatoes, salt, paste, stock, potatoes, and garlic to the pot. Bring to a boil, stir, cover, and reduce heat. Simmer for one hour or until vegetables are just barely tender.
4. Add pasta and let simmer over heat for another 30 minutes. Season further as taste requires.
5. Serve topped with cheese!

Tools: *Mixing Bowl, Skillet, Wooden Spoon*

DIFFICULT: BEGINNER **SERVES: 4**

LEMON CHICKEN SKILLET

INGREDIENTS

- 1 lb. chicken breasts
- 1 lemon, sliced thin
- 2 tsp. chopped fresh parsley
- 1 sprig fresh thyme
- 2 T butter
- Season as desired

DIRECTIONS

1. Warm a skillet over medium heat and season chicken breasts with salt and pepper.
2. Cook the breasts over medium heat for 6-8 minutes until an internal temperature of 165°F or 75°C is reached.
3. Melt butter in pan and drop in a sprig of thyme. Place the lemon slices and thyme on top of the breasts and spoon the melted butter onto the chicken to moisten it.
4. Top with chopped parsley and serve!

Tools: *Chef's Knife, Skillet, Spatula, Wooden Spoon*

DIFFICULT: BEGINNER   **SERVES: 4**

STEAK FAJITAS

INGREDIENTS

- 1 lb. flank or skirt steak, sliced
- 1 T cornstarch
- 2 tsp. chili powder
- 1 tsp. salt
- 5 tsp. pepper
- 1 tsp. paprika
- 5 tsp. onion powder
- 5 tsp. garlic powder
- 25 tsp. cayenne pepper
- 5 tsp. ground cumin
- 1 green bell pepper, seeded and sliced
- 1 red bell pepper, seeded and sliced
- 5 red onion, thinly sliced

DIRECTIONS

1. Heat the skillet over medium heat.
2. In a small bowl, combine all herbs and seasonings, before mixing well.
3. Using about half the seasoning mixture, season the steak on both sides and cook about 3-4 minutes per side until fully cooked. Let rest for 10 minutes, then thinly slice.
4. In the same skillet, add a little bit of oil if needed, then sauté onions and peppers with remaining seasoning.
5. Serve meat and veggies on tortillas with your choice of toppings!

Tools: *Chef's Knife, Skillet, Spatula, Wooden Spoon*

DIFFICULT: BEGINNER **SERVES: 6**

CHICKEN FRIED RICE

INGREDIENTS

- 1 lb. chicken breasts
- 2 T olive oil
- Season as desired
- 1.5 c. frozen peas and carrots
- 1 med. onion, diced
- 3 cloves garlic, minced
- 1 T ginger, minced
- 4 c. white rice, cooked and cooled
- 3 lg. eggs, beaten
- 3 T soy sauce
- 2 green onions, thinly sliced

DIRECTIONS

1. Warm a skillet or wok over medium heat and season chicken breasts with salt and pepper.
2. Cook the breasts over medium heat for 6-8 minutes until an internal temperature of 165°F or 75°C is reached. Move to cutting board and cut into chunks or thin slices.
3. Add veggies to skillet or wok. Once soft, add garlic and ginger. Stir in rice and mix.
4. Make a well in the center of the rice and pour in eggs. Stir to cook, then add chicken and soy sauce, stirring thoroughly.

Tools: *Chef's Knife, Large Skillet or Wok, Spatula, Wooden Spoon*

DIFFICULT: BEGINNER   **SERVES: 4**

WHOLE ROASTED CHICKEN

INGREDIENTS

- 1 whole chicken, cleaned and patted dry
- .25 c unsalted butter, melted
- 3 T olive oil
- 2 tsp. dried rosemary
- .5 tsp. pepper
- 4 cloves garlic, minced
- 1 tsp. salt

DIRECTIONS

1. Ensure your oven is on and heated to 450°F or 220°C.
2. In a small bowl, mix butter and seasonings, then top chicken with it, rubbing it into the skin. Make sure to get the spots around the joints!
3. Bake in the oven for one hour or until an internal temperature of 165°F or 75°C is reached.
4. Slice and serve!

Tools: *Baking Dish*

CHAPTER 4:
SNACK RECIPES

DIFFICULT: BEGINNER **SERVES: 6**

CHEESY CRACKERS

INGREDIENTS

- 25 tsp. salt
- 5 c. all-purpose flour
- 5 tsp. paprika
- 5 tsp. vegetable oil
- 75 c. lightly packed shredded sharp cheddar cheese
- 1 T cold water, or as needed
- 1/3 c. lightly packed shredded parmesan cheese
- 2 T unsalted butter, softened

DIRECTIONS

1. Line a cookie sheet with foil and spray with non-stick spray.
2. In a mixing bowl, combine cheeses, paprika, and salt. Mix with the rubber spatula until thoroughly combined.
3. With a fork, mix in the flour until the mixture is crumbly. Sprinkle in a drop or two of water at a time and mix with a spatula until a dough forms that holds its shape when squished.
4. Transfer the dough to a clean work surface like the counter and press until it makes a big, flat patty. Wrap in plastic place in the refrigerator and chill 30 minutes.
5. Ensure your oven is on and heated to 375°F or 190°C and flour your work surface.
6. Roll your dough out to about 1/8th of an inch thick and cut even shapes out of the dough. If you have small cookie cutters, you can use them to make fun-shaped crackers! Using a skewer, poke 5 small holes into each cracker.
7. Bake for 15 minutes, or until crisp. Let stand for one hour and serve!

Tools: *Cookie Sheet, Mixing Bowl, Rolling Pin, Rubber Spatula*

DIFFICULT: BEGINNER **SERVES: 1**

CHEESE QUESADILLA

INGREDIENTS

- 1 flour tortilla
- 2 oz. shredded cheddar cheese

DIRECTIONS

1. Over medium heat, heat a skillet and add oil or non-stick spray to prevent sticking.
2. Once the pan is hot, lay your tortilla into the pan and place the cheese on one half of it.
3. Using your spatula, fold the other half of the tortilla over and let the quesadilla sit for 1-2 minutes until a golden brown crisp forms.
4. Flip the quesadilla and heat for another 1-2 minutes.
5. Slice and serve!

Tools: *Skillet, Spatula*

DIFFICULT: BEGINNER   **SERVES: 4**

PIZZA PULL-APART RING

INGREDIENTS

- 5 pkg. pizza dough
- 4 oz. pepperoni
- 4 oz. mozzarella
- A pinch of dried oregano
- 4 T jarred pasta sauce

DIRECTIONS

1. Ensure your oven is on and heated to 375°F or 190°C.
2. Using your hands, flatten the dough out into a circle about 8 inches wide.
3. Spoon the sauce into a circle and layer pepperoni and cheese onto it.
4. In the center, cut an asterisk (*) and pull the points up over the pizza filling. Pull the outer edges of the dough up to meet the points and pinch each to secure it. Some of the filling will be exposed.
5. Bake for 15 minutes until the top has taken on a golden quality brown and serve!

Tools: *Cookie Sheet, Paring Knife*

DIFFICULT: BEGINNER   **SERVES: 1**

NACHOS

INGREDIENTS

- 1-2 oz. tortilla chips
- 1-2 oz. shredded cheddar cheese
- 1 T chunky salsa
- Pickled jalapeno slices (optional)

DIRECTIONS

1. Ensure your oven is on and heated to 325°F or 165°C.
2. Line a cookie sheet with foil and spray with non-stick spray.
3. Layer tortilla chips on the sheet, close together without too much overlap. Sprinkle cheese over top and place jalapenos evenly throughout, according to taste.
4. Bake in the oven for one ten minutes or until the cheese bubbly and melted.
5. Top with salsa and serve!

Tools: *Cookie Sheet*

DIFFICULT: BEGINNER   **SERVES: 12**

SPINACH DIP

INGREDIENTS

- 1 packet vegetable soup mix, powdered
- 8 oz. sour cream
- 8 oz. mayonnaise
- 16 oz. cut leaf spinach, frozen, thawed, and drained

DIRECTIONS

1. In a medium mixing bowl, combine all ingredients and stir for 2-3 minutes, or until all the spinach has been broken up and evenly spread through the dip.
2. Cover and refrigerate for at least two hours before serving.
3. Serve with chunks of sourdough bread or with white corn tortilla chips!

Tip: Even if you don't like spinach, this dip is delicious!

Tools: *Mixing Bowl, Rubber Spatula*

DIFFICULT: BEGINNER **SERVES: 1**

GRANOLA

INGREDIENTS

- 5 c. honey
- 5 c. vegetable or canola oil
- 5 tsp. ground cinnamon
- 5 tsp. salt
- 1 c. raisins or other dried fruit
- 1 c. sliced almonds
- 3 c. rolled oats

DIRECTIONS

1. Ensure your oven is on and heated to 300°F or 150°C. And line a cookie sheet with parchment paper.
2. In a large bowl, combine oil, honey, cinnamon, and salt. Whisk until completely combined.
3. Add oats and almonds and stir until completely coated.
4. Bake for 20 minutes, stopping at 10 minutes to stir the granola on the parchment. This helps with even cooking.
5. Add fruit to the granola and allow to cool completely before eating

Tip: If you want clumpy granola with big chunks, use your spatula to push down on the granola to mush it together a little bit before you set it out to cool.

Tools: *Cookie Sheet, Mixing Bowl, Parchment Paper, Whisk*

DIFFICULT: BEGINNER   **SERVES: 4**

SMOKY SNACK MIX

INGREDIENTS

- 25 tsp. cayenne (optional)
- 1 tsp. smoked paprika
- 2 c. mixed nuts of your preference
- 3 c. mini pretzels
- 3 T brown sugar
- 4 T butter, melted

DIRECTIONS

1. Ensure your oven is on and heated to 325°F or 165°C. Line a cookie sheet with parchment paper or foil.
2. In a small bowl, combine butter, sugar, paprika, and cayenne. Stir until combined.
3. In a large bowl, combine nuts, pretzels, and butter mixture. Toss or stir until coated completely.
4. Pour snack mix onto the cookie sheet and spread into one, even layer with little overlapping.
5. Bake at 325°F or 165°C for 20 minutes, stirring occasionally for even cooking.
6. Let cool completely and serve!

Tools: *Cookie Sheet, Mixing bowls, Parchment Paper, Rubber spatula*

DIFFICULT: BEGINNER **SERVES: 8**

NUTELLA POCKETS

INGREDIENTS

- 1 can pizza dough
- 1 egg, beaten
- 2 oz. granulated sugar
- 8 oz. Nutella (if you want to prepare it at home you can follow the recipe Hazelnut spreadable cream - Homemade Nutella. Download the EXTRA RECIPES pack)

DIRECTIONS

1. Preheat the oven to 400°F or 200°C and line a cookie sheet with foil. Spray with non-stick spray.
2. Roll out pizza dough to about .25 of an inch thick and cut out circles that are about three inches wide.
3. In each circle, put a dollop of Nutella.
4. Brush the edges with the egg and fold the pizza dough in half to make a half-moon-shaped pocket around the chocolate. Use your fingers to pinch the dough shut.
5. Brush the tops of each pocket with egg, then dust with sugar.
6. Poke a small hole in the top of each pocket, then bake for 20 minutes at 400°F or 200°C, until the top has taken on a golden quality brown.
7. Let cool for five to ten minutes and serve!

Tools: *Cookie Sheet, Foil, Pastry Brushm, Rolling Pin, Spoon*

DIFFICULT: BEGINNER SERVES: 8

OATMEAL COOKIES

INGREDIENTS

- 1.5 tsp. ground cinnamon
- 1 c. brown sugar, packed
- 1 c. butter, softened
- 1 c. granulated sugar
- 1 tsp. baking soda
- 1 tsp. salt
- 1 tsp. vanilla extract
- 2 c. all-purpose flour
- 2 eggs
- 3 c. quick oats

DIRECTIONS

1. In a medium mixing bowl, cream together butter and sugars. Once creamed, add eggs one at a time and then mix in the vanilla.
2. In a separate bowl, combine flour, salt, baking soda, and cinnamon before mixing well. Mix into the creamed butter and sugar and then add oats. Stir until the texture is mostly uniform and a dough forms. Cover the bowl place in the refrigerator and chill one hour.
3. Preheat the oven to 375°F or 190°C and line a cookie sheet with foil. Spray with non-stick spray.
4. Rub a little olive oil onto your hands, then pull out little pieces of dough, rolling them into balls. You want each ball to be about an inch wide. Flatten each ball of dough onto the cookie sheet so it looks like a cookie. If you'd like, you can top each cookie with a little bit more granulated sugar.
5. Bake for 8-10 minutes, let cool completely before serving!

Tools: *Cookie Sheet, Foil, Mixing Bowl, Wooden Spoon, Whisk*

DIFFICULT: BEGINNER **SERVES: 6**

HARD-BOILED EGGS

INGREDIENTS

- 12 eggs, raw and uncracked
- Water
- Salt

DIRECTIONS

1. In a large pot, place all your eggs gently, then fill with water until each egg is about 1 inch underwater.
2. Sprinkle a very generous portion of salt into the water and put the pot over high heat to bring the water to a boil.
3. Once boiling, cover the pot and turn off the heat and let stand for 11 minutes.
4. Remove from the hot water and transfer eggs into an ice bath. Let stand another 10 minutes, then peel and serve!

Tools: *Large pot, Mixing Bowl*

CHAPTER 5:
DESSERT RECIPES

DIFFICULT: INTERMEDIATE **SERVES: 6**

CHOCOLATE MOUSSE

INGREDIENTS

- 1 5 c. whipping cream, chilled
- 25 c. cocoa powder, sifted
- 25 tsp. vanilla extract
- 5 c. powdered sugar

DIRECTIONS

1. Chill your mixing bowl by either placing it in the freezer for 15-20 minutes or by letting it sit with ice water in it for 10 minutes. Be sure to completely dry your bowl before you use it!
2. In your chilled mixing bowl, whip your whipping cream with your hand mixer until frothy and slightly thick.
3. Add powdered sugar and cocoa powder and mix carefully with your whisk until soft peaks form in your mixture.
4. Add in your vanilla extract and continue to whip until stiff peaks form.
5. Chill for one hour, then serve!

Tools: *Hand Mixer , Mixing Bowl, Whisk*

DIFFICULT: BEGINNER **SERVES: 8**

SIMPLE VANILLA ICE CREAM

INGREDIENTS

- 2 c. heavy whipping cream
- 1 can (14 oz.) sweetened condensed milk
- 1 tsp. vanilla extract

DIRECTIONS

1. In a mixing bowl (large), use a hand mixer to whip the cream until you get stiff peaks.
2. In another bowl, whisk together the vanilla and condensed milk until there are no more swirls of color showing in it.
3. Gently fold the whipped cream into the condensed milk, taking care to keep the texture intact.
4. Pour the mixture into the container and freeze for 4-6 hours.
5. Top with whatever you love and serve!

Tip: You can make whatever flavors you like with this base! Just add new flavor extracts and toppings to see what you can make!

Tools: *Container, Hand Mixer, Mixing Bowls, Rubber Spatula, Whisk*

DIFFICULT: BEGINNER   SERVES: 8

PEACH COBBLER

INGREDIENTS

- 5 c. butter
- 1 c. granulated sugar
- 1 c. milk
- 1 c. self-rising flour
- 2 cans (16 oz.) sliced peaches in heavy syrup

DIRECTIONS

1. Preheat the oven to 350°F or 175°C and spray baking dish with non-stick spray.
2. Mix flour, sugar, and milk together with as few lumps as possible.
3. Pour mixture into the baking dish, then top with peaches and syrup. Spread evenly.
4. Bake for 30-40 minutes, or until the crust turns golden brown.
5. Let cool for five to ten minutes and serve!

Tip: Best when topped with a scoop of vanilla ice cream!

Tools: *Baking Dish, Mixing Bowl, Rubber Spatula, Whisk*

DIFFICULT: BEGINNER **SERVES: 8**

BERRY COBBLER

INGREDIENTS

- 4 T butter
- 75 c. all-purpose flour
- 75 c. granulated sugar
- 1 tsp. baking powder
- 25 tsp. salt
- 75 c. milk
- 12 oz. frozen berries
- 1 T granulated sugar

DIRECTIONS

1. Preheat the oven to 350°F or 175°C.
2. Once the oven is preheated, set the butter in the baking dish and put the dish in the oven. Allow butter to melt, then remove the pan from the oven.
3. Mix dry ingredients (except for the 1 T granulated sugar), then add milk and whisk until the batter is smooth.
4. Pour batter into the baking dish, then top with frozen berries. Spread evenly.
5. Top with remaining tablespoon of granulated sugar.
6. Bake for 50-60 minutes, or until the crust turns golden brown.
7. Let cool for five to ten minutes and serve!

Tip: Best when topped with a scoop of vanilla ice cream!

Tools: *Baking Dish, Mixing Bowl, Rubber Spatula, Whisk*

DIFFICULT: INTERMEDIATE **SERVES: 8-10**

DOUBLE LAYER CHOCOLATE CAKE

INGREDIENTS

- 5 c. vegetable oil
- 75 c. butter
- 75 c. unsweetened cocoa powder
- 1.5 c. unsweetened cocoa powder
- 1.5 tsp. baking powder
- 1.5 tsp. baking soda
- 1.75 c. all-purpose flour
- 1 c. boiling water
- 1 c. milk
- 1 tsp. salt
- 1 tsp. vanilla extract
- 2 c. granulated sugar
- 2 eggs
- 2 tsp. vanilla extract
- 6 c. milk
- 5 1/3 c. powdered sugar

DIRECTIONS

1. Preheat the oven to 350°F or 175°C and spray cake pans with non-stick spray.
2. In a mixing bowl, combine sugar, .75 c of cocoa, flour, baking soda, baking powder, and salt. Once mixed, add the oil milk, eggs, and vanilla. Mix for 3 minutes until there are no lumps, then stir in the boiling water by hand. Divide batter between two pans.
3. Bake for 30-35 minutes or until an inserted toothpick comes out clean.
4. Make frosting by creaming remaining ingredients. Once the cake cools, frost it, cut into slices and serve!

Tools: *2 Cake Pans, Hand Mixer, Mixing Bowl, Rubber Spatula, Whisk*

DIFFICULT: INTERMEDIATE **SERVES: 8-10**

PEARS CAKE

INGREDIENTS

- 1 1/4 c. vegetable oil
- 1 c. pecans, chopped
- 1 c. pecans, chopped
- 1 tsp vanilla extract
- 5 c. butter, softened
- 5 tsp. salt
- 2 c. all-purpose flour
- 2 c. granulated sugar
- 2 tsp. baking powder
- 2 tsp. baking soda
- 2 tsp. ground cinnamon
- 2 tsp. vanilla extract
- 1 lb. pears (finely cutted)
- 4 c. confectioners' sugar
- 8 oz. cream cheese, softened

DIRECTIONS

1. Preheat the oven to 350°F or 175°C and spray baking dish with non-stick spray.
2. In a mixing bowl, combine eggs, oil, granulated sugar, and 2 tsp. vanilla extract. Mix in the flour, baking powder and soda, cinnamon, and salt. Fold in pears and pecans, then pour into dish.
3. Bake for 40-50 minutes or until an inserted toothpick comes out clean.
4. In a medium bowl, cream the remaining ingredients to make a frosting.
5. Frost the cake, slice, and serve!

Tools: *Baking Dish, Hand Mixer, Mixing Bowl, Rubber Spatula, Whisk*

DIFFICULT: INTERMEDIATE **SERVES: 8-10**

WALNUTS COOKIES

INGREDIENTS

- 1 c. butter (softened)
- 1 c. walnuts (chopped)
- 1 c. brown sugar, packed
- 1 c. granulated sugar
- 1 tsp. baking soda
- 5 tsp. salt
- 2 c. semisweet chocolate chips
- 2 eggs
- 2 tsp. hot water
- 2 tsp. vanilla extract
- 3 c. all-purpose flour

DIRECTIONS

1. Preheat the oven to 350°F or 175°C.
2. In a mixing bowl, cream together the butter and sugars until smooth.
3. Beat in one egg at a time, then stir in the vanilla.
4. In hot water, dissolve the baking soda, then add to cookie dough along with salt.
5. Stir in the flour and walnuts.
6. On a cookie sheet, lay down spoonfuls of cookie dough, 1-2 inches apart.
7. Bake for about 10 minutes, or until the edges are nicely browned.
8. Let cool for five to ten minutes and serve!

Tip: Best with a glass of milk!

Tools: *Cookie Sheet, Mixing Bowl, Rubber Spatula, Whisk*

DIFFICULT: INTERMEDIATE **SERVES: 10**

CHOCOLATE CHIP SNICKERDOODLES

INGREDIENTS

- 1 5 c. granulated sugar
- 1 tsp. baking soda
- 5 c. butter, softened
- 5 c. shortening
- 25 tsp. salt
- 2 .75 c. all-purpose flour
- 2 eggs
- 2 T granulated sugar
- 2 tsp. cream of tartar
- 2 tsp. ground cinnamon
- 2 tsp. vanilla extract
- 2 c. chocolate chips

DIRECTIONS

1. Preheat the oven to 400°F or 200°C.
2. In a bowl, cream together 1 .5 c of granulated sugar, eggs, butter, shortening, and vanilla. Once creamed, stir in the flour, chocolate chips, cream of tartar, baking soda, and the salt.
3. Put a little oil on your hands to prevent the dough from sticking, then using a spoon, pull bits of the dough out of the bowl and roll into 1-inch balls.
4. Place pieces of dough about 2 inches apart on cookie sheets and bake for 8-10 minutes. You want your cookies to be set, but not too hard.
5. Once your cookies have been removed from the oven, take the cookies off the pans so they don't continue to cook.
6. Let cool for five to ten minutes and serve!

Tools: *Cookie Sheet, Mixing Bowl, Rubber Spatula, Whisk*

DIFFICULT: BEGINNER   **SERVES: 8**

NO-BAKE CHEESECAKE

INGREDIENTS

- 1 can (14 oz.) sweetened condensed milk
- 1 graham cracker pie crust
- 1 tsp. vanilla extract
- 11 T unsalted butter, melted
- 2 pkg. (8 oz. each) cream cheese, room temperature
- 2 T granulated sugar

DIRECTIONS

1. In a medium mixing bowl, use your hand mixer to beat the cream cheese until completely smooth. A little bit at a time, add the condensed milk, then add the vanilla extract and continue to mix until thoroughly combined. Make sure to use your rubber spatula as you mix, bring more of the filling mixture to the center of the bowl.
2. Pour the filling into the pie crust and smooth the top with the rubber spatula.
3. Cover and refrigerate for up to 3 hours, or until firm.
4. Slice and serve!

Tools: *Hand Mixer, Mixing Bowl, Rubber Spatula, Whisk*

DIFFICULT: BEGINNER **SERVES: 9**

STRAWBERRY SHORTCAKE ICEBOX CAKE

INGREDIENTS

- 4 c. heavy cream
- 5 c. powdered sugar (plus extra for dusting, if desired)
- 2 tsp. vanilla extract
- 1.5 boxes vanilla wafer cookies
- 1 lb. strawberries, thinly sliced

DIRECTIONS

1. In a large bowl, beat together the heavy cream, vanilla, and powdered sugar until medium peaks form.
2. You're going to layer the ingredients like a lasagna. Coat the bottom of the pan with a thin layer of whipped cream (it's okay if you can see through it here and there), then put down an even layer of vanilla wafers. Top with strawberries. Repeat cream, cookies, berries two more times or for as many layers as you have room and ingredients.
3. Top the cake with one final layer of cream and berries.
4. Refrigerate until the cookies get nice and soft, about 2-3 hours or up to overnight.
5. Sprinkle with more powdered sugar if desired, then serve!

Tools: *Baking Dish, Hand Mixer, Mixing Bowl, Rubber Spatula*

CHAPTER 6: IDEAS FOR MORE COOKING FUN

When you're looking for new recipes to try, you're going to want to look at all the possible resources that are available to you for finding them. Cookbooks are a great way to go, because you can look at a cookbook with a specific theme or type, you can look for a specific cuisine you like, or if there's a chef that you admire, you can get all the tips they have to offer. Popular chefs who have been on Food Network shows, or who you may know have all made cookbooks and may have more recipes that you would like to try.

There are so many cookbooks, chefs, and recipes out there, so keep your eyes open for the flavors, proteins, presentations, cooking methods, and skills that excite you. There will always be something new to learn in the kitchen and knowing as much as you can know is never a bad thing.

If you're looking into other recipes, you might want to consider looking into some of the more classic dishes that are known and try to master some of those. Food doesn't have to be difficult in order to be delicious, so just keep that in mind as you continue to search through recipes.

If you find that you like to cook, but you're not interested in recipes that take several hours and several different methods of cooking to complete, then you're not alone and there's nothing wrong with that. Never feel like your passion for cooking has to take you to places that you don't enjoy. Millions of people all over the world love to cook and learn how to make new flavor combinations to wow their friends and family, but you don't have to break the bank or go outside of your comfort zone to do those things. Here are some other dishes you can learn how to make!

Baked Macaroni and Cheese – This is a classic dish that can be served at just about any gathering, whether its friends, family, coworkers, a boy scout troop, or just about anything else. It's hearty, it's delicious, and it's got a baked crisp on top that just makes it so much better than a stovetop macaroni and cheese. Now, this can be a little bit harder than you might think, so don't be disappointed if your first batch doesn't come out exactly perfect. Considering trying to make smaller batches of it to test the recipes that you find, so you can see which one you like the best. You might find that a recipe that uses one kind of cheese just isn't your kind of thing, and you might find that you like your macaroni and cheese with a bit more flavor than is considered traditional. There is nothing wrong with any of that! Just make sure you don't make a huge batch of a recipe you don't care for!

Baked Ziti – This is an Italian classic that is actually a good deal simpler than you might think. It's funny that baked ziti has about the difficulty level you would expect macaroni and cheese to have, and macaroni and cheese has about the difficulty level you would expect from macaroni and cheese. The wonderful thing about baked ziti is that you will usually make much more than you could ever eat in one night, so you have plenty of leftovers to reheat throughout the week. And because it's such a delicious recipe, you will find that you don't mind having it for dinner for a few nights in the week!

Banana Bread – A very simple recipe with very few ingredients, that is always just a shade tastier than you remember it being. Sure, it's not chocolate cake or anything, but if you like bananas, it's a really great flavor that you can't help but enjoy. Make your banana bread with or without walnuts, top it with icing, warm it up and eat it with a little bit of butter on top, or simply munch on it along with a glass of milk or a c of tea. Banana bread is one of those recipes that makes a great gift as well. If you don't know what to get someone, surprising them with a loaf of banana bread is great.

Beef Stew – This is a classic dinner recipe because it's delicious, it has meat, vegetables, and starch in it, and it's a rib-sticking meal. That means you won't be hungry just a short while after eating it like you might with some leaner, less satisfying meals. You never have to worry about that with something like a hearty beef stew.

You can find recipes that take hours and hours and hours to make, or you can find recipes that only take about 20-30 minutes to make. It all depends on how much time you have, how much time you want to spend, and what ingredients you would like to use. Such a delicious and filling recipe is so versatile makes it a great go-to if you don't know what to make for dinner, especially if it's cold out!

Blueberry Muffins – These are great because you can keep them on hand for a quick breakfast addition, a nice snack, or you could even have them for dessert if you like them well enough. And like just about every other baked good you can think of, they make a great gift. Got a new neighbor that you'd like to get to know, but you don't know how to get the conversation started? Make them some blueberry muffins and bring them over in a nice basket. That's sure to make them feel welcome to the neighborhood. Be sure to bring an adult with you!

Brownies – One of the most classic baked goods you could ask for. These make a great addition to any party, gathering, meeting, bake sale, or weekday. They're very simple to make (especially with a store-bought mix), and they're absolutely delicious. If you're not a big fan of cakes, but you like brownies, you can cook brownies in a muffin tin and bring those to school for your birthday instead! They're great and just about everyone loves them. You can add nuts if you like them in your brownies, you can frost them with any flavor or color you love, you could add sprinkles that fit your favorite theme, or you can simply have them with nothing on them and they're still absolutely delicious. Save me a corner piece!

Chicken Casserole - Chicken casserole varies in ingredients, depending on who you ask, so you will likely be able to find at least one chicken casserole recipe that you love. The casserole is an American institution. It's a staple of American home cooking because they don't take a lot of prep work, they don't have overly complex ingredients in them, you bake them once for up to an hour, and then dinner is ready. They're perfect for someone who is starting out with cooking, someone who doesn't like to do a whole lot of moving around the kitchen, someone who would like dinner prep to be fast and easy, or someone who has a lot of people to feed all at once.

Chicken Noodle Soup - This is a classic recipe for when you're feeling sick, but it's also a great comfort food for a cold night. It's a hearty and delicious soup that usually has white meat, noodles, chicken, and celery. You can make your own additions to the recipe as you see fit, and you can change the flavors if you're not particularly fond of the classic chicken broth flavor. You're bound to find a recipe that you love and, once you do, you will keep it close to your heart and make it every time someone in your life gets sick. You won't be able to keep yourself from doing it.

Chicken Pot Pie – Chicken Pot Pie is another American classic dinner food. It's easy to make a ton of it for very little in terms of cost and prep work. For some, the classic peas and carrots mix inside a pot pie just isn't appealing, which is what makes home cooking so great. You can substitute the fillings in chicken pot pie for just about anything when you're cooking at home for yourself because you're in complete control! You can add some tomato paste to it and change it from a classic creamy pot pie to one that's more robust in flavor, you can just change out the vegetables inside, you could make changes to the crust, or anything else you'd like to change. Before you know it, you've got a completely custom recipe that you thought up all by yourself.

Cinnamon Buns – A breakfast classic that is served at many breakfast bars and restaurants, and which makes an appearance at just about any good brunch there is. Depending on how you would like to make your buns, or depending on how much effort you would like to expend in getting them, you can find an option that will work for you. There are delicious cinnamon buns that come premade and sliced, which you can just put into a ban, bake, ice, and serve. There are premade doughs that allow you to make your own filling, roll, slice, bake, and ice, your buns or you can make them completely from scratch if that's something that you would rather do!

Dutch Baby – This one might be a little bit less common, but it is a classic. This is a dessert or breakfast pastry that is cooked and baked in a cast-iron skillet. If you have seen one, you know they're not much to look at, but they taste pretty wonderful. They're a simple, sweet dessert that is great for a group. Sure, you could eat a whole one by yourself, but you might give yourself a tummy ache and, like most foods, it tastes best when you can share it with someone.

Eggs Benedict – **Most kids might give this one a pass, but it's a very delicious and classic breakfast. This a poached egg over seared Canadian bacon or ham, on top of an English muffin and topped with hollandaise (a very rich, creamy, and delicious sauce) and served with hash browns. Usually, you get two eggs, two pieces of ham, and two muffins, but some places do just one. You can make that in your own home and wow whoever was lucky enough to be home for the occasion! It is a dish with a few different steps of cooking and prep, so it might be something you want to work toward, but if you're into it and you'd like to do the work, the flavor and satisfaction this meal delivers are well worth the effort.**

Empanadas – **These are not an American classic, but they are nonetheless delicious. These are little dough pockets that are usually filled with meat and vegetables, but you can fill them with just about anything you'd like to fill them with. Some restaurants have gotten clever and filled them with sweet, cinnamon apples. It's like a mini, handheld apple pie. Classic empanadas though can even be a little bit spicy if that's something that you like. You might find that, as you eat more spicy foods, that you gain a liking for them, or that you have a better tolerance for the heat.**

Flaky Buttermilk Biscuits – **These are another American classic that can go with just about any meal of the day. With breakfast, they make great sandwiches, they're great with sausage gravy, they're a perfect accompaniment to fried chicken, or just about any other southern food that you can possibly think of. If you're looking to be super healthy and eat little fat and carbs, these are not the right things to get. If you're looking for something yummy that you can make pretty easily to go along with something else you've made, these are just about as perfect as you can possibly get!**

Garlic Bread – **Some of the recipes in this list would go along perfectly with garlic bread. You can make a lot of changes to garlic bread so it fits your needs and wants, so don't feel like you're stuck with what's in the frozen aisle at the grocery store. You can make garlic bread out of a crusty artisanal loaf, you can use a soft French bread, you can make your own garlic butter with your favorite herbs, or you can buy one that is premade. You can add cheese, or you can have it without cheese. It's all up to you, and pretty much anything you choose is going to be absolutely delicious, so don't worry!**

Hamburgers – **If you like hamburgers at restaurants, but you're not a huge fan of them at home, I have a tip for you! Your burger patties are too thick. Make patties that are slightly wider and about half as thick, Cook these thin patties until they get a nice crisp around the edges, then add whatever burger toppings you like to add the most. This type of patty is called a smash burger since they're smashed onto the grill or pan and there's nothing wrong with liking them more! Since they're half the thickness of what you're used to at home, you can make double cheeseburgers without making a mess or having**

trouble.

Jalapeno Poppers – These are more simple to make than you might think, so don't worry! These are usually jalapenos that have been cored and seeded, filled with cheese or cream cheese, then breaded and fried. You can make all sorts of variations on this recipe as well. You can stuff jalapenos with cream cheese, wrap them in bacon, and then bake them if you're not into the whole fried food thing, or you could try something completely different as well. They make such a great party appetizer, or as a side with a meal. Anyone who likes a little spice will usually love these.

Lasagna – Lasagna is a classic dinner dish that will satisfy your hunger like a professional. It's packed with meat, pasta, and cheese. So, honestly, what's not to like about a lasagna! They do take a lot of work if you're not used to making them. You need to make layer after layer of meat, cheese, and pasta, with can take some time, but the dish will feed a lot of mouths and will be well worth the time it takes to prep and cooks. This is another dish that is perfect with some garlic bread and a nice fresh side salad to go along with it. Dish out a slice and dig in!

Meat Pie – Meat pies can be made with many different fillings, pastry doughs, and can even be made in just about any size you can think of. If you don't like a classic meat pie, consider changing the gravy that goes into it, choosing a meat that you love, and some vegetables that really get you going. Making a muffin tin full of little meat pies is a great way to feed a crowd and to please them all. These are hearty little pies that will keep your guests tided over until dinner begins, or you can make a slightly bigger one and then it is dinner!

Meatloaf – Some people don't like meatloaf, and some people think it's absolutely delicious. The population is divided on this, but if it's something you like, it's definitely worth learning how to make it. The ingredients are fairly simple and just like lasagna, you get a lot of servings out of one recipe. Having leftovers for yourself to use for dinners or lunches, or being able to feed a large group of people is the aim of a lot of family chefs. It might not be your goal, though. So be sure you're looking at the servings for each recipe that you make. If you end up with more food than you will eat, be smart about your portions! Consider giving extra portions away to friends and family so it doesn't go to waste, or consider freezing them and eating them next week!

Pizza – You can get just about as creative or in-depth with pizza as you would like. There are pre-made, frozen pizzas you can bake, there are pre-made crusts you can top and bake, there are pre-made doughs you can roll out, top, and bake, or you can make your pizza dough from scratch. Making pizza at home is such a fun activity because you can put just about anything on it that you love. If you like ham and pineapple on your pizza, go nuts. If you're more of a pepperoni and bacon kind of person, have at it. If you're someone who likes all the veggies, then this pizza is your personal playground! Making your own pizza at home isn't something that typically leaves you with a lot of leftovers or anything, but it's so delicious, that it's something you can usually overlook.

Quiche – This is one of those recipes that a lot of kids might not care for, as it's got spinach and egg in it, but it is far more delicious than you might think. It's a pastry pie crust filled with a delicious mixture of eggs, cheese, and vegetables. If you're not big on spinach, but you feel like you would like all of the rest that quiche has to offer, then you can customize! Just keep an eye on it while it's in the oven and make sure you're not leaving it in the oven for too long to cook what you put in it. Having an overdone quiche is no fun, but it's still bound to be delicious with all that cheesy goodness in there. Have fun with it!

Roasted Turkey – Picture it now: you in charge of the family's next holiday meal. With a little chef like you in the house, who needs professionals! Let mom put her feet up while you brine, stuff, and dress the turkey for her next holiday season. While you're at it, you can probably make a quiche, a baked macaroni and cheese, and maybe a green bean casserole if you've got time! Don't forget to make the mashed potatoes, rolls, and candied yams as well. Okay, maybe you don't have to do all of that, but wouldn't it be cool if you knew how to make the biggest part of your next holiday dinner?

Shawarma – This is another classic that isn't American, but it is certainly absolutely delicious. Flavorful chicken, lamb, or beef that is usually served on pita with vegetables and a very flavorful seasoning rub over the lot. With a creamy yogurt sauce to go along with it, it's a lot of new and intense flavors that you might really enjoy.

Shepherd's Pie – Some people make this with lamb, but a lot of people choose to use ground beef for this dish. It's almost like a casserole with a layer of deliciously seasoned meat, peas, and beautifully browned mashed potatoes over top. It's all baked together until it gets nice and crisp on top, then it's served like any other casserole. This is another dish that would benefit from a biscuit or two on the side to dip in the gravy and mashed potatoes.

Sloppy Joes – You wouldn't believe how simple it is to make these. You can buy sauce to pour over browned meat, you can make your own seasoning, or you can buy seasoning packets to turn ground meat into sloppy joes. Whichever way you prefer is the way you should go, there is no right or wrong. You could also see if you can make any changes to the classic sloppy joe so it's something a bit more than you remember it being.

Zucchini Bread – This might not sound so great at first, but I promise you that zucchini bread is way more delicious than it sounds. It's a lot like banana bread in that it's pretty easy to make and it's a wonderful gift to give out to those you like in your life. Consider making some for the next party you have and see how your friends like it!

CHAPTER 7: COOKING IDEAS TO DO TOGETHER

As mentioned in the previous chapter, there are some recipes that might scare you off because they're a lot of work. While it's perfectly okay to be disinterested in something that would take too much work for too little pay-off, you might want to consider that some of those recipes might be ideal for cooking with one or more other people to help you. If you can divide the tasks evenly between you, you might find that it's easier to make the things that you want to make!

Baked Spaghetti – This takes a few different steps between making the pasta, making the sauce, layering it into a baking dish with cheese, and then baking it. The time might go by much faster with the help of a friend or family member. Baked Spaghetti makes a lot of servings for each recipe, so you can have a few helpers and still have plenty to go around, no matter how hungry everyone is. This can be a little bit of a dense meal, so you'll want to have something like a side salad to brighten things up a little and to keep things from sitting quite so heavily in your stomach.

Beef Stew – Beef stew isn't a particularly difficult or involved dish to make, but there are some vegetables in it that need chopping. If one of you takes one of the vegetables and the other one takes on another, then the chopping is done in mere minutes! Then it's just a matter of putting everything in the pot and waiting or it all to be done! The hardest part of making beef stew is having to smell it in your house without eating it before it's all the way done. Get a nice hearty, crusty bread to dunk in your stew and it's just about the best meal you can get for a cold winter night.

Burgers – Burgers aren't hard to make, but everyone can chip in to make their own patties, sliced onions, lettuce, and tomatoes for topping, or they can slice the cheese if you'd like some of that on top of your patty. Sometimes, it can be fun to make unique sauces to put on the burger as well. You're not just limited to ketchup and mustard. Try some barbecue sauce, maybe some mayo, maybe some steak sauce or whatever else you happen to have on hand. Burgers are a great meal to be creative with because the flavors lend themselves so well to other styles of cuisine.

Chicken Curry – This meal is a little bit more complex, so with the help of your friends or family, you should be able to knock it out of the park! It's a lot easier than you think. Some plain or Greek yogurt, the right curry powder or mix, chicken, onion, cilantro, and rice? That's a delicious meal right there. Add some tomato and ginger for a little bit of Tikka Masala. There are so many different types of chicken curry, so be sure to look around for new types, variations, flavors, and components to add to your own. If there's something you don't like about a curry, chances are that there is a different one that will fit your tastes better.

Chicken Fricassee – This is a slightly more advanced cooking method, but with the help of a friend or family member, you should be able to pull it off. It's a rich and delicious dish that is sure to impress just about anyone you have for dinner. You can make this for your family and they'll be so shocked at how far you've come in learning how to cook! You don't have to tell them that it's really a lot easier than the dish looks like it would be. You can let them think you're a young master chef!

Chicken Paprikash – This is another dish with a fairly involved cooking process that might seem a little bit daunting at first, but it's absolutely delicious and you should definitely be able to make it through the recipe with the help of a family member or a friend helping you to get all the steps done. Don't get overwhelmed. If you feel like the dish is going to be too difficult when you read the recipe, look at the steps and try to imagine how you could do them. If you can't, simply wait a little while, cook some other things, then come back to it and see if it seems a little more doable.

Chicken Quesadillas – A cheese quesadilla is one thing. Adding fillings makes it a whole new ball game and the dish becomes a whole meal! It's not necessarily hard to make them, but if you're having a party or if you and your family like to cook together, each of you could make your own quesadilla, just like you like it. You could have bowls of each ingredient set on the counter for each person to pick from and they can load up their quesadilla, then cook them on the stovetop! It only takes a couple of minutes to make a quesadilla, since all the ingredients are pre-cooked, but the cooking before this step may require helping hands!

Cookies – Baking cookies with friends and family is a great way to spend an evening! This is especially true if you're making your cookies from scratch like you would with the recipes in the desserts section of this book. There are a number of steps that people can help with and rolling out and cutting dough can make your arms tired after a while. Having someone to cut off about half of them and roll them out for you can be a big help, and it's always nice to have someone to share them with when you're all done making them!

Corned Beef Hash – Corned beef hash, or any other type of hash, could seem like a little bit too much effort with having to dice up the potatoes really small, get them cooked to perfection, and then do the same thing with the meat. But if you have help, it takes no time at all and it's delicious. Some people like to use leftover roast beef, ham, bacon, breakfast sausage, or other meats that they like. A hash is just diced potatoes, meat, and possibly other vegetables if you want to add them. You can make a hash without too many ingredients, then put a fried egg on top for a hearty, delicious breakfast.

Eggs Benedict – Most kids might give this one a pass, but it's a very delicious and classic breakfast. This a poached egg over seared Canadian bacon or ham, on top of an English muffin and topped with hollandaise (a very rich, creamy, and delicious sauce) and served with hash browns. Usually, you get two eggs, two pieces of ham, and two muffins, but some places do just one. You can make that in your own home and wow whoever was lucky enough to be home for the occasion! It is a dish with a few different steps of cooking and prep, so it's definitely something that could benefit from having helpers. The flavor and satisfaction this meal delivers are well worth the effort.

Enchiladas – Enchiladas are a delicious food that takes a bit of work. You need to cook the chicken and other fillings, roll them into tortillas, then lay them in a baking dish on top of enchilada sauce, cover with cheese and more enchilada sauce, then bake for a little while. It's a bunch of steps, but with more hands, you should be able to get the enchiladas rolled and baked without a problem. Plus, they're just an absolutely delicious meal with some rice and a nice fresh salad. You'll feel like your own home is a restaurant when you sit down to eat them.

Fish and Chips – This is battered fish that has been fried and served alongside French fries. You can cut and batter the fish while a family member fries them in the hot oil, or you can buy pre-battered ones to bake yourself. You can do the same with French fries, as you can bake or fry frozen French fries, or you can cut your very own from real potatoes if that's something you'd like to do. This is a classic dish from England that is usually made with cod or another white fish, and it's quite delicious. You can enjoy them with ketchup, tartar sauce, cocktail sauce, or even a little salt and malt vinegar.

French Bread Pizzas – If you're having some people over, making French bread pizzas can be a great group activity. Everyone can layer their preferred ingredients onto the pizzas, bake and eat! Just like with the quesadillas, you can set out ingredients for everyone to use, then they can all get cooked at once. You can put things like cheese, sauce, pepperoni, sausage, peppers, onions, black olives, or whatever you like best on your pizzas. Because the French bread pizzas go on only a portion of a loaf, it's possible to get four or even six pizzas out of one French bread loaf.

Fried Chicken – Fried chicken can be very simple to make at home, but it's best to have an adult supervising or taking care of the frying because hot oil is a serious business. You can make a batter or a dredge for your fried chicken and, within minutes, you have your very own homemade fried chicken with delicious crispness and flavor. It can take a lot of work, though, which makes it a good group activity. This is one of those recipes that is best done with an adult or two, so they can help you with food safety and with getting the chicken to the right level of doneness. Don't forget to use a meat thermometer to check it before you bite into it.

Goulash – This is a classic, hearty dish made with ground meat, vegetables, and macaroni or cavatappi pasta. It's rib-sticking, delicious, savory, and it'll warm you right up. It's almost like a thick tomato stew with pasta, and if you make a big batch of it, you can use the leftovers for a week. This is a good thing to cook with more than one person because you might need help cutting up the vegetables, browning the meat, and cooking the pasta so it's all done at the right times. An adult can help you to time everything so your goulash comes together wonderfully.

Jambalaya – This is a classic, spicy dish. If you don't like spice, you will have a little bit of a challenge with making this dish without it. Most Jambalaya recipes call for "Cajun seasoning," which is a blend of herbs and spices that contains cayenne pepper. If you would like to make your own seasoning mixture, however, you can cut out the spicy parts and you can leave out the jalapeno. This dish is perfect for more than one person to make because you need bell peppers, onion, sausage, shrimp, and chicken. Having helping hands to make the prep work go a little faster will certainly help things along!

Mashed Potatoes – Cooking potatoes is pretty simple, but cutting them can be tiring work if you've never done it before. They're very thick vegetables that it can take some muscle to get through. You just need to cut them up into chunks, boil them for 15-20 minutes or so, then you need to mash them with either a mixer or a masher. If you don't have a mixer, then you will need to use a masher, which can take a lot of time, patience, and muscle. If you've never made mashed potatoes by yourself before, you might want to have an adult on standby to take over when you need to give your arms a little bit of a break.

Monkey Bread – This is also known as "pull-apart bread." This is usually made with canned biscuit dough that is rolled up into a bunch of little balls, then baked in a Bundt pan with a sugary syrup and chocolate chips throughout. It's delicious, but making all those little balls of dough can take a long time. More (clean) hands make light work out of it and at the end of it, you have something delicious to share. Consider getting some cool whip to dip the chunks into. It's absolutely delicious.

Pie – If you're making your own pie crust, it can help to have some people to help you out. Sometimes dough can be hard to roll out on your own, and with all the other parts of the pie to bring together, it might help to have more than one person working on it together. If you're using a pie crust, then you and your cooking buddy can just work together to make the most delicious filling you can. Whether it's apples with cinnamon, pumpkin, cherry, blueberry, or whatever else you can imagine, the pie is always easier with friends.

Pizza – The pizza can be fun to make together because you can make more than one pizza for yourselves to have, or you can share the pizza and split which ingredients go on either side. If you do more than one pizza, everyone can layer their preferred ingredients onto the pizzas, bake and eat! Just like with the quesadillas, you can set out ingredients for everyone to use, then they can all get cooked at once. You can put things like cheese, sauce, pepperoni, sausage, peppers, onions, black olives, or whatever you like best on your pizzas.

Ravioli – Ravioli is a pasta with a lot of steps. It requires that you make the dough, chill it, roll it out, fill it, crimp it, and then cook it. It can take a lot of effort, but if you put the right things into your ravioli, then it will be absolutely delicious. You can fill it with things like meat, cheese, vegetables, or a mixture of all three if that's what you'd like to do.

Stuffed French Toast – In this book, you got two recipes for how to make some French toast dishes. This is another one that's great to do with people because you need a loaf of unsliced bread, to be sliced into really thick slices. You then have to make a cut in the center of the bread, stuff it what you want (usually sweetened cream or cream cheese), batter it, then fry it. It's an absolutely delicious dish, but it's more work than you might like to do if it's just you at the breakfast table. Not to worry, it's always okay to put your diners to use in the kitchen and make them work for their meal!

Tacos – Tacos were described in one of the recipes in this book and it's not necessarily hard to make them, but if you're having a party or if you and your family like to cook together, each of you could make your own tacos, just like you like them. You could have bowls of each ingredient set on the counter for each person to pick from and they can load up their taco, then cook them on the stovetop! It only takes a couple of minutes to make a quesadilla, since all the ingredients are pre-cooked, but the cooking before this step may require helping hands!

Vegetable Soup – The reason vegetable soup makes a good group activity is because of the prep that goes into getting a vegetable ready to go into the pot. If everyone takes a vegetable and cuts it up just right, then in no time, the pot will be full and ready to simmer!

"KID CHEF COOKING" CONCLUSION

Thank you for making it through to the end of *Young Chef Cookbook: The Complete Cooking Book for Kids Who Love to Cook and Eat*, let's hope it was informative and able to provide you with all of the tools you need to achieve your goals whatever they may be.

The next step is to try each of the recipes in this book and test your cooking skills. You will want to make sure that you try lots of new things in the kitchen to discover new flavors, new recipes, new foods, and to push the boundaries of what you know.

Cooking is such a great passion to have and there are so many resources out there for you to use. Always look out for new skills that you can learn to make your time in the kitchen more fun and more rewarding.

INTRODUCTION TO "KID CHEF BAKING"

Congratulations on purchasing *Kid Chef: Young Chef Cookbook - The Complete Baking Book for Kids Who Love to Bake and Eat* **and thank you for doing so!**

The following chapters will discuss everything you need to know about baking so you can make delicious meals for your friends and family. These recipes are sure to impress and satisfy anyone who comes to your table. In these chapters, you will find all the information you will need to go from a beginner's understanding of baking and how it works to an intermediate level that will allow you to prepare a large meal for everyone you love to enjoy! Whether you're looking to learn how to bake muffins for a friend or make a flatbread pizza, this book can help you to get the information you need. The information in this book will fill you with confidence and allow you to try all sorts of new and delicious things. If you're looking for some good reasons to learn how to bake, here some great ones!

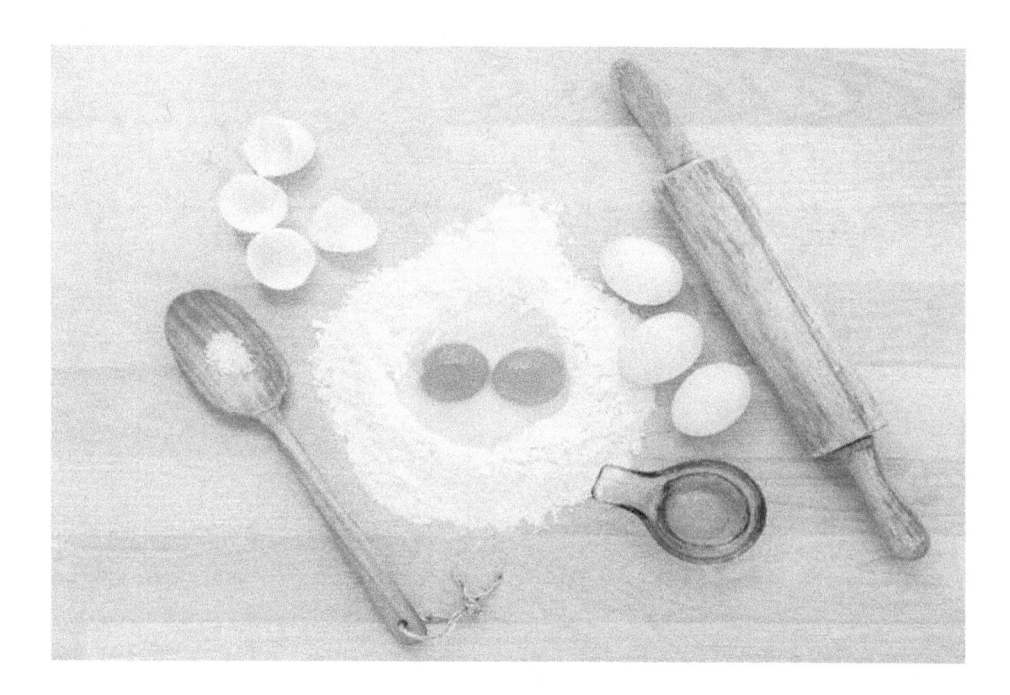

CHAPTER 1: BAKER'S TOOLS

Baking Dishes – **There are many dishes that you might want to cook in the oven. A ceramic dish that is deeper than your average cookie sheet or baking pan is the perfect tool for such a job and should be kept on hand if you like to make delicious meals for the whole family in the oven.**

Blender – **This might be one of the more seldom-used tools, but it's one of those things that you can't really come up with a replacement or substitute for when you're in a pinch and need one, so many chefs like to keep them on hand for when they need them. You can use a blender to even out the texture of a soup or a sauce, you can use it to make a base for something, and it's just the best tool for what it does.**

Cake Tins – **Baking a cake can really only happen in a cake tin. Baked goods take on the shape of the container they're in if they're rising, and you want something that is as uniform as possible.**

Can Opener – **Opening cans with a sticky or rusty can opener can slow down your whole rhythm when cooking, so it's best to get a can opener that can glide right through and open cans with ease.**

Cookie Sheets - **These are a classic, and they usually come in packs of three. You will need these for sheet pan recipes as well as cookies.**

Cutting Board – **Don't cut your meat, fruit, and vegetables on the bare counter, or you'll scuff up the counters and dull your knives! Get a cutting board made of wood, resin, or plastic that will help keep your prep work safe and hygienic.**

Food Processor – **This might be one of the more seldom-used tools, but it's one of those things that you can't really come up with a replacement or substitute for when you're in a pinch and need one, so many chefs like to keep them on hand for when they need them. You can use a food processor to grind meat, make guacamole, chop up veggies into rough pieces, and so much more.**

Grater – **A classic cheese grater can be used for so many more things than just cheese. You can use grated things in many different recipes, so don't discount their use.**

Hand Mixer – **When you're putting together a thick mixture, a hand mixer can mean the difference between five minutes and thirty. When flour starts to bind with liquid and fat, it can get tough, or when potatoes need quick and smooth mashing, it can take a long time. A hand mixer cuts that work in half.**

Kitchen Shears – These are large kitchen scissors that are very sharp. They are meant to cut through the thin backbones of chicken, the leaves of an artichoke, and so much more. Kitchen shears can make quick work of a lot of tasks.

Knives – Any chef will tell you that their knives are their most prized tools. A basic chef's knife is a good place to start, and you will find more knives with more uses as you gain experience and get better with them.

Mixing Bowls – Mixing bowls help you to get a batter or a dough together in the right amounts. Other bowls in the kitchen just aren't big enough.

Paring Knife – This will help you to make small decorative cuts in your pastry or to make the small, precise cuts needed on some baked goods.

Pie Pans – When you're making a pie, nothing is quite like a pie pan, as it's got slanted edges that make it nice and easy for the delicate crust to form.

Rolling Mat – While these aren't completely essential, it is nice to have a rolling mat for easy cleanup, as well as to tell you how big your dough is.

Rolling Pin – You can use other things in the kitchen to roll out your dough, but at the end of the day, the rolling pin is just the best tool for the job. Don't forget to flour it!

Rubber Spatulas – Rubber or silicone spatulas are helpful because they make complete contact with the side of the bowl and can completely scrape all the batter or contents out for you. It makes washing those big mixing bowls so much easier!

Saucepan – A medium saucepan will be called for in a large number of recipes that you'll find.

Spatula – Every chef needs a spatula! You can't even cook an egg or get your cookies off the cookie sheet without a spatula, so this is one of the very bare basics every chef needs.

Strainer – Whether you choose to go with a fine-mesh sieve or colander, you will need a way to remove water or liquid from your dishes at some point or another. Colanders are typically used for draining pasta, and sieves are used for rinsing rice before cooking, but both have many uses.

Thermometer – A meat thermometer or kitchen thermometer can tell you how far along your cooking is coming and how soon you will need to pull things off or out of the heat.

Timer – Most chefs will need a reminder when their time is up for things that are being cooked, especially if it's in the oven. Out of sight, out of mind, and you don't want your food in the oven to go out of mind!

Tongs – These are a precision tool that allows you to pick things up and flip or move them with ease. These can help you to do a lot of things and make the kitchen work a lot easier.

Vegetable Peeler – Whether you're peeling carrots, potatoes, apples, or something else, these make that work so much easier. Pros can use paring knives; peelers are much more precise and faster.

Whisk – A whisk can sometimes be substituted for a fork, but a good whisk can help you whip up things that a fork generally can't. This tool is found at most chef's stations.

Zester – You can't really zest with any other tool in your kitchen with the exception of maybe the paring knife and the grater. A zester is far faster and easier to use, though, so that is more highly recommended.

CHAPTER 2: BREAKFAST BAKING RECIPES

PREPARATION+COOK TIME: 30 M

SERVES: 6

A Dutch Baby is essentially a giant pancake but with a flair and style that the pancake lacks.

DUTCH BABY

INGREDIENTS

- A half-cup of flour
- A quarter teaspoon of salt
- 2 eggs
- A single teaspoon of vanilla
- A single lemon
- 3 tablespoons of butter that is unsalted
- A single tablespoon of sugar
- A single cup of milk
- A single tablespoon of powdered sugar garnish for the dish

DIRECTIONS

1. Make sure that your oven is preheated to 400 degrees F.
2. Get yourself a bowl.
3. Get a whisk.
4. You will need to use the whisk and whisk the milk and flour together until it has become smooth and then add in your eggs along with your vanilla, sugar, and salt.
5. Whisk them all together and make sure they combine before setting them aside.
6. Get a skillet that is safe for the oven.
7. Place the butter in the skillet.
8. Put the skillet in the oven after making sure that you have preheated it in step
9. Watch the pan very closely and make sure that when the butter is sizzling that you pour batter into your pan.
10. Shut the door and do not open it.
11. Allow your Dutch Baby to cook for 17 minutes.
12. Remove from the oven and garnish with powdered sugar.
13. Cut into it however you like, and it's ready for you to eat.

Nutritional: *Calories-140, Fat-8 grams, Carbs-12 grams, Protein-5 grams, Fiber-1 gram*

PREPARATION+COOK TIME: 30 M **SERVES: 8**

QUICHE

Quiche is a great meal that is easy to make and will yield a lot of leftovers. It's great for meal planning and testing your abilities as a chef. Many consider it to be a meal of formal occasions, but these days everyone makes them.

INGREDIENTS

- A half teaspoon of salt
- A single cup of shredded cheese (use cheddar)
- A quarter teaspoon of pepper
- A whole wheat pie crust that measures 9 inches
- ¾ of a cup of milk (use whole milk)
- 5 eggs (large)
- 2 cups of florets of broccoli

DIRECTIONS

1. Make sure that your oven has been preheated to 375 degrees F.
2. Roll out your crust if it doesn't have a shape.
3. Chill the crust until you need to use it.
4. Get a small pot.
5. Place a minimum of one cup of water and a maximum of two cups of water into the bottom of the pot.
6. Add in your broccoli and then cover your pot.
7. Bring to a boil.
8. Cook your broccoli until it is tender and crispy. This will take 4 minutes.
9. Move your broccoli from the pot to a colander.
10. Rinse with cool water and make sure it drains thoroughly.
11. Carefully chop broccoli into pieces that are small.
12. Get a large bowl.
13. Get a whisk.
14. In the bowl, you will need to whisk together your milk, pepper, and salt, along with your eggs.
15. Get your broccoli and stir it in along with the cheese.
16. Pour mixture into the pie shell that has been prepared.
17. Bake the quiche for a minimum of 35 minutes and a maximum of 40 minutes.
18. The eggs should be set in the middle.
19. You should check on the quiche at the 25-minute mark. If you notice that the crust is browning too quickly, you will need to tent it with foil.
20. Let it stand for a solid 5 minutes before you serve it.

Nutritional: *Calories-228, Fat-16 grams, Carbs-12 grams, Protein-10 grams, Fiber-2 grams*

PREPARATION+COOK TIME: 1 H **SERVES: 6**

Muffins are a staple for breakfasts, and they make a tasty snack for other parts of the day as well. As a chef adding muffins to your arsenal is a must.

BLUEBERRY SWIRL MUFFINS

INGREDIENTS

- 2 and a half cups of flour (use all-purpose)
- 2 cups of divided blueberries
- A single teaspoon of granulated sugar
- 2 eggs (use large)
- 4 tablespoons of butter that is unsalted and has been melted and cooled
- A quarter cup of vegetable oil
- A single cup of buttermilk
- A cup and ⅛ of granulated sugar
- 2 and a half teaspoons of baking powder
- A single teaspoon of table salt
- A teaspoon and a half of

DIRECTIONS

1. Adjust one of the oven racks to an upper-middle position, and be sure to heat your oven to 425.
2. Get yourself a cupcake pan with a dozen cups.
3. Line the pan.
4. Set your pan to the side.
5. Get a saucepan.
6. Add in a single teaspoon of sugar along with a single cup of blueberries and bring to a simmer. The heat should be set to medium to accomplish this.
7. Smash your berries until they have thickened and reduced to a quarter cup about 6 minutes.
8. Get a small bowl and place the mix in it.
9. Let cool for a quarter of an hour.
10. Get a large bowl.
11. Get a whisk.
12. Use the whisk and whisk the salt, flour, and baking powder together.
13. Get a smaller bowl that is of medium size.
14. Use the whisk again on the eggs and remaining sugar and whisk them until combined and nice and thick.

INGREDIENTS

vanilla extract

For the topping:
- A teaspoon and a half of grated lemon zest
- A third of a cup of granulated sugar

DIRECTIONS

15. Whisk in the butter but do this slowly and whisk in the oil slowly until they too have combined.
16. Whisk in the vanilla and buttermilk as well until they have combined.
17. Get a spatula made of rubber.
18. Fold the egg mixture in and the remaining berries to the flour mixture until moistened.
19. It is important that you don't over mix here. You want the batter lumpy in a few spots and have a few spots of dry flour remaining as well.
20. Use a spoon and place the batter in the prepared cupcake pan.
21. Fill the cups completely and mound slightly.
22. Place a teaspoon of the berry mix you cooked to the center of each cup.
23. Use a toothpick to give it the swirl design.
24. Sprinkle the topping you made over the top.
25. Bake for 18 minutes. The muffins should be a golden brown, and if you shove a toothpick in the middle, it should come out clean or with very few moist crumbs attached.
26. It helps to rotate the pan at the halfway mark.
27. Let cool for 5 minutes and place on a wire rack for an additional 5 minutes of cooling.

Nutritional: *Calories-293, Fat- 9 grams, Carbs-49 grams, Protein-4 grams, Fiber- 1 gram*

PREPARATION+COOK TIME: 2 H 15 M   **SERVES: 12**

CINNAMON BUNS

Cinnamon buns should be a decadent and delicious meal that makes you feel like you have just had dessert.

INGREDIENTS

How to make the icing:
- A single cup of sugar that is powdered
- 4 ounces of room temperature cream cheese
- 2 tablespoons of milk
- A single teaspoon of vanilla extract that is pure
- 2 tablespoons of butter that has been melted

For the rolls themselves:
- A single egg (use large) that will be lightly whisked
- Cooking oil spray
- A quarter of a teaspoon of salt
- 3 and a half cups of all-purpose flour

For the yeast:
- A single cup of milk that has been warmed to the touch. Do not make it hot.
- 2 and a half teaspoons of yeast that is a quick rise
- 5 tablespoons of sugar that is granulated
- A quarter of a cup of butter that has been melted

For the filling:
- 2 tablespoons of butter that has been melted
- half a cup of brown sugar that has been loosely packed
- 2 tablespoons of cinnamon (you will need to use the ground in this case)

DIRECTIONS

How to make the icing:
1. A single cup of sugar that is powdered
2. 4 ounces of room temperature cream cheese
3. 2 tablespoons of milk
4. A single teaspoon of vanilla extract that is pure
5. 2 tablespoons of butter that has been melted

For the rolls themselves:
6. A single egg (use large) that will be lightly whisked
7. Cooking oil spray
8. A quarter of a teaspoon of salt
9. 3 and a half cups of all-purpose flour

For the yeast:
10. A single cup of milk that has been warmed to the touch. Do not make it hot.
11. 2 and a half teaspoons of yeast that is a quick rise
12. 5 tablespoons of sugar that is granulated
13. A quarter of a cup of butter that has been melted

For the filling:
14. 2 tablespoons of butter that has been melted
15. half a cup of brown sugar that has been loosely packed
16. 2 tablespoons of cinnamon (you will need to use the ground in this case)

Nutritional: *Calories-322, Carbs-46 grams, Protein-6 grams, Fat-12 grams, Fiber-1 gram*

PREPARATION+COOK TIME: 15 M **SERVES: 20**

BACON CHEESE BREAD

Bacon cheese bread is both delicious and filling and leaves you completely satisfied. It is great for parties or when you feel like something savory for yourself.

INGREDIENTS

- A loaf of French bread that is 14 ounces
- A single tablespoon of dip mix (go with ranch)
- ¾ of a cup of mayonnaise
- 2 cups of cheese that has been shredded
- 4 slices of baked bacon that has been crumbled

DIRECTIONS

1. Preheat your broiler.
2. Cut your bread in half (do this lengthwise).
3. Line your baking sheet with a foil that is nonstick.
4. Get a bowl.
5. Combine your bacon, cheese, mayo, and ranch in the bowl.
6. Use a spatula to spread your cheese on both halves of the bread.
7. Place under your broiler for 8 minutes until it turns a golden brown.
8. Before you cut it, let it cool slightly.

Nutritional: *Calories-168, Carbs-11 grams, Protein-5 grams, Fat- 10 grams*

PREPARATION+COOK TIME: 40 M **SERVES: 12**

Popovers are a great treat, and most of the time, people eat them with jam, but this is a dish that you can get really creative with. This recipe, for example, is for a cheesy popover.

POPOVERS

INGREDIENTS

- A single cup of warm milk
- 2 eggs (large)
- A quarter of a teaspoon of salt
- A half teaspoon of black pepper (use cracked)
- 3 tablespoons of butter that has been melted
- A single cup of flour (use all-purpose)
- 2 tablespoons of parmesan (grated finely) and add a little for the top of the popover

DIRECTIONS

1. Make sure your oven is preheated to 425 F.
2. Place a muffin pan inside as it preheats.
3. Get a bowl.
4. Get a whisk.
5. In the bowl, whisk your parmesan, spices, eggs, and milk together.
6. Add in your flour and mix it just enough so that the lumps are gone.
7. When your oven is at the appropriate temperature, get your muffin pan (carefully, don't burn yourself), and brush 8 of the spots with your butter that you melted. (if your pan only has 8 spots then you will need to do this again to make another four for a full dozen)
8. Scoop enough batter into each spot so that it reaches almost the top of your pan.
9. Sprinkle cheese on top.
10. Put the pan in the oven.
11. Bake 20 minutes and turn down your heat to 350 before baking an additional ten minutes.
12. You can serve right away.

Nutritional: *Calories-75*

PREPARATION+COOK TIME: 25 M

SERVES: 5

Huevos Rancheros is a wonderful dish that is both cultural and delicious at the same time. Recipes for this meal have flavors that explode on the tongue, and ours is no different.

HUEVOS RANCHEROS

INGREDIENTS

- 10 eggs (large)
- half a cup of queso fresco that has been crumbled
- 2 avocados ripe and sliced
- 10 flour tortillas (we recommend Old El Paso)
- 2 tablespoons of oil (vegetable)
- 15 ounces of black beans
- 15 ounces of chorizo (use Mexican)
- Ranchero Sauce

You can also add extra ingredients if you like, but you should be aware of the fact that it will change the nutritional information

DIRECTIONS

1. Warm your sauce on your stove.
2. Pour your beans in a pot that is small (a saucepan is a good option here).
3. Your heat should be medium when you are warming this, and you need to heat until simmering before turning the heat off.
4. Get a skillet that is nonstick and large in size and put the chorizo inside it.
5. Set the heat to medium-high.
6. Break the chorizo apart and then brown it. This should take about ten minutes.
7. Your chorizo should be starting to be crispy, and you will need to put it on a plate.
8. Wipe your skillet down (a paper towel is fine)
9. Add 2 tablespoons of the oil and set it back over that same medium-high heat that you had before.
10. Add your tortillas a single one at a time. You want them to puff for about 5 seconds before you flip them and then repeat the process.
11. After you do this, remove the tortillas and then set them on paper towels to drain. Repeat this process until all of your tortillas are golden and puffy.
12. In the same skillet, you cooked everything else in and cooked the eggs 'to order.'
13. Place the ingredients on the tortilla.

Nutritional: *Calories-1019, Carbs-60 grams, Protein-47 grams, Fat-65 grams, Fiber-14 grams*

PREPARATION+COOK TIME: 30 M **SERVES: 4**

BREAKFAST PIZZA

Do you love pizza? "Then you'll love this! It's the perfect starter for your day.

INGREDIENTS

- A single handful of spinach (use baby spinach)
- 8 sliced cherry tomatoes
- 4 large eggs
- A single cup and 5 ounces of all-purpose flour (you can also use white whole wheat flour)
- 2 strips of chopped and cooked center cut bacon
- 2 ounces and a half cup of mozzarella cheese (shredded)
- Half a teaspoon of salt (kosher)
- A teaspoon and a half of baking powder
- A single cup of Greek yogurt (use nonfat and make sure it has no liquid)

DIRECTIONS

1. Make sure that your oven is preheated to 450 F.
2. Get a baking sheet and place a silicone liner on it.
3. Get a bowl.
4. Combine your salt and baking powder along with the flour and whisk them together well.
5. Add in your yogurt and use a fork to mix it. It should be combined well, and you should be able to see small crumbles in the mix.
6. Dust flour lightly on a flat surface and then remove your dough from the bowl.
7. Knead the dough for almost 2 dozen turns. Your dough should be tacky and not leave anything on your hand.
8. Separate the dough into four balls.
9. Sprinkle the flat surface with flour and do the same to a rolling pin.
10. Roll until you have an oval that is 8 inches in its diameter.
11. Place on the baking sheet.
12. Top with cheese, and your spinach, as well as your tomatoes, but leave a hole in the middle open. This is where you're going to put the egg.
13. Break an egg and place it in the middle of the dough (gentle when you break), and then put the bacon on top.
14. Bake for 12 minutes. Your crust should be golden. The egg should be set.
15. Season the dish.

Nutritional: *Calories-271, Carbs-27 grams, Protein-20.5 grams, Fiber-1.5 grams, Fat-9 grams*

PREPARATION+COOK TIME: 45 M **SERVES: 12**

Breakfast casserole is another dish that is easy to make, good for practicing, and makes plenty of food.

BREAKFAST CASSEROLE

INGREDIENTS

- Half of a teaspoon of pepper
- 2 cups of milk
- 2 pounds of breakfast sausage (hot)
- 8 eggs
- 2 cups of cheddar cheese that is shredded
- A single bag of shredded hash browns that are frozen and 30 ounces

DIRECTIONS

1. Make sure that your oven is preheated to 350.
2. Get a large skillet.
3. Cook the sausage until there is no pink anywhere to be found.
4. Drain your fat.
5. Add your hash browns to your skillet and cook them until they have turned slightly brown.
6. Place those hash browns in a pan that is 9 by 13 and greased lightly.
7. Place your sausage and cheese over the top.
8. Get a whisk.
9. Whisk together your spices, milk, and eggs.
10. Pour this over the top of the other ingredients in the pan.
11. Bake for 40 minutes.

Nutritional: *Calories-632, Fat-46 grams, Carbs-26 grams, Fiber- 3 grams, Protein-24 grams*

PREPARATION+COOK TIME: 1 H 5 M   **SERVES: 18**

FLAKY BUTTERMILK BISCUITS

Buttermilk biscuits are a staple in most homes. Particularly in certain cuisines. This recipe is a good one to have your disposal as a chef.

INGREDIENTS

- A single cup of buttermilk
- 3 cups of flour that is all-purpose
- 4 teaspoons of sugar
- A single teaspoon and a half of salt (kosher)
- 8 teaspoons of baking powder
- A dozen tablespoons of butter (this amounts to a stick and a half). They will need to be cut into pieces that are half an inch and chilled.

DIRECTIONS

1. Get a bowl.
2. Combine your sugar and salt with your flour and baking powder.
3. Get a whisk.
4. Whisk these items together until you find that the mixture has combined well.
5. Add the pieces of butter that you sliced.
6. Use your fingers and rub the flour mix until half of the butter has combined thoroughly. The remaining half should be in small pieces and some bigger sized pieces, but none should be bigger than a hazelnut.
7. Add in your buttermilk.
8. Mix it together with a spatula and do this until the dry ingredients have just moistened.
9. Add in additional milk if needed but do it one tablespoon at a time.
10. On a flat surface, lightly dust your space with flour, then place your dough on it and press it until it forms a rectangle.
11. Fold this in half and turn the dough 90 degrees.
12. Flatten it again.
13. Repeat this process until you have four.
14. You will know when it's the proper look when it is fairly smooth.
15. Roll your dough until it is a quarter-inch thick.
16. Get a biscuit cutter.
17. Use it to cut as many biscuits as possible.
18. Place these biscuits on a sheet pan that has been lined with parchment.
19. Place the pan in the fridge for a half-hour.
20. Use the extra dough to make more biscuits (the scraps).
21. Heat your oven to 350 F.
22. When the biscuits are done in the fridge and put them in the oven.
23. Bake for 20 minutes. The bottoms should be golden brown and firm.

Nutritional: *Calories-165, Fat-9 grams, Protein-2 grams, Carbs-18 grams*

CHAPTER 3: MAIN COURSE BAKING RECIPES

PREPARATION+COOK TIME: 2 H 30 M **SERVES: 8**

ROASTED WHOLE CHICKEN WITH ROOT VEGETABLES

Nutritious and delicious. This is a great dish for any chef to learn and become familiar with.

INGREDIENTS

- A whole chicken (four pounds)
- 2 tablespoons of fresh rosemary (you need it to be finely chopped and an additional three sprigs for the cavity)
- A single tablespoon of fresh sage (chopped and four additional sprigs for the cavity)
- A single teaspoon and a half of red pepper flakes
- 6 tablespoons of olive oil
- 2 tablespoons of fresh thyme (chopped finely and 3 additional sprigs for the cavity)
- 4 carrots (slender and peeled)
- The zest of a single lemon and a half of a lemon
- 2 garlic cloves that are grated finely (you need the remaining head of garlic, and you will need to halve it in a horizontal manner to expose the cloves in each half)
- 2 bay leaves
- A single turnip that is medium in size (you need to peel it and cut it into ¾ inch pieces)
- A single pound of rutabaga (peel it and cut it into ¾ inch pieces. Cubes will look aesthetically pleasing. Don't eat or use the leaves at all)

DIRECTIONS

1. Make sure your oven is preheated to 375 F.
2. Place your chicken on a baking pan that is rimmed.
3. Get a small bowl.
4. Place the pepper flakes, garlic, zest, rosemary, sage, thyme, oil, a single teaspoon of salt, and two of the pepper in the bowl. Stir everything to make sure that it is combining.
5. Rub your chicken completely with half of the herb oil. Make sure that you get some under the skin of the thighs and breasts.
6. Stuff the cavity with your sprigs of thyme, rosemary, and sage, along with your bay leaves, half lemon and garlic head halves that you made.
7. Place your veggies in a bowl.
8. Toss the veggies in the remaining oil mixture.
9. Place the veggies around the chicken and put it in the oven.
10. Roast until the vegetables have become tender, and the chicken has been cooked through. You will be able to tell it's done with a thermometer that is instant-read and insert it into the thickest part of the thigh. It should read 160 degrees F at around the time of an hour and 15 minutes.
11. Let it sit for 10 minutes before you carve it.

Nutritional: *Calories-564, Fiber-3 grams, Fat-35 grams, Protein-51 grams, Carbs-12 grams*

PREPARATION+COOK TIME: 1H 15 M **SERVES: 2**

CHICKEN POT PIE

Chicken pot pie is a classic, and it's been around forever. Many find it comforting and make it people happy when they eat it.

INGREDIENTS

- A single teaspoon of thyme (dried)
- A single cup of cubed butter
- 2 cups of potatoes that are peeled and diced
- ⅔ of a cup of onion that is chopped
- A single cup of peas that are frozen
- A cup of corn that is frozen
- 3 cups of chicken broth
- A single cup of all-purpose flour
- A single cup and ¾ of carrots that are sliced
- 4 sheets of pie crust (refrigerated)
- ¾ teaspoon of pepper
- A single teaspoon and ¾ of salt
- A single cup and a half of whole milk
- 4 cups of chicken (cooked and cubed)

DIRECTIONS

1. Make sure that your oven is preheated to 425.
2. Place your carrots and potatoes in a saucepan.
3. You will need to add water to cover.
4. Bring it to a boil.
5. Reduce your heat and then cover and cook for 10 minutes.
6. They should be tender and crispy.
7. Drain.
8. Get a large skillet.
9. Heat your butter over a heat that is medium-high.
10. Add in the onion and cook it until it's tender. Don't forget to stir.
11. Stir in the seasonings and the flour until it has blended.
12. Slowly stir in your milk and broth before bringing it to a boil. Stir constantly here.
13. Cook and stir it for an additional 2 minutes.
14. It should be thickened now.
15. Stir in your potato, corn, chicken, and peas mix and remove from the heat.
16. Unroll your pie crust into a 9-inch pie plate. Trim, so it's even with the rim of the plate.
17. Add in the chicken mix.
18. Unroll the other crusts and place over your filling.
19. Trim it and seal it.
20. Flute the edges.
21. Cut slits in the tops.
22. Bake for 40 minutes, and you should see a crust that is lightly browned.
23. Let it stand for a quarter of an hour before you cut it.

Nutritional: *Calories-475, Fat-28 grams, Carbs-41 grams, Protein-15 grams, Fiber- 2 grams*

PREPARATION+COOK TIME: 1 H

SERVES: 4

Savory and very filling this is another dish that is a good start for becoming a great chef.

BAKED ZITI

INGREDIENTS

- A single onion that has been chopped
- 2 jars of spaghetti sauce (26-ounce jars)
- A single pound of ziti pasta (dry)
- A single pound of ground beef that is lean
- A single cup and a half of sour cream
- 2 tablespoons of parmesan cheese that is grated
- 6 ounces of provolone cheese that has been sliced
- 6 ounces of mozzarella cheese that has been shredded

DIRECTIONS

1. Get a large pot.
2. Bring a pot of water that has been lightly salted to a boil.
3. Add pasta and cook till al dente. This is for approximately 8 minutes.
4. Drain it.
5. Get a skillet.
6. In the skillet brown the beef and onion over a heat of medium.
7. Add the sauce and simmer for a quarter of an hour.
8. Preheat your oven to 350.
9. Get a baking dish that is 9 by 13.
10. Butter the baking dish.
11. Layer the dish with half of the ziti, provolone cheese, sour cream, half of the sauce mix, the remaining ziti and then the mozzarella and the rest of the sauce.
12. Top with the parmesan.
13. Bake a half-hour, and the cheese should be melted.

Nutritional: *Calories-578, Fat-25.3 grams, Carbs-58.4 grams, Protein-27.9 grams*

PREPARATION+COOK TIME: 1 H **SERVES: 4**

SHEPHERD'S PIE

Quiche is a great meal that is easy to make and will yield a lot of leftovers. It's great for meal planning and testing your abilities as a chef. Many consider it to be a meal of formal occasions, but these days everyone makes them.

INGREDIENTS

- A single tablespoon of butter
- A single tablespoon of onion that has been chopped finely
- 4 potatoes that are cubed, peeled and large in size
- A quarter cup of cheddar cheese that has been shredded
- 5 chopped carrots
- A single chopped onion
- A single pound of ground beef that is lean
- 2 tablespoons of flour (use all-purpose)
- A single tablespoon of vegetable oil
- A single tablespoon of ketchup
- A quarter cup of cheddar cheese that is shredded
- ¾ of a cup of broth that is beef

DIRECTIONS

1. Get a large pot and add salted water to it before bringing it to a boil.
2. Add your potatoes and cook them until they are firm but tender. This should take a quarter of an hour.
3. Drain it before mashing it.
4. Mix in your butter and the onion that is finely chopped along with a quarter cup of the cheese that is shredded.
5. Season and place to the side.
6. Bring a large pot of water that has been salted to a boil and add your carrots. Cook them for a quarter of an hour until firm but tender.
7. Drain and mash them before setting aside.
8. Heat your oven to 375 F.
9. Heat your oil in a frying pan.
10. Add your onion and cook it until it's clear.
11. Add beef and cook until it has been browned well.
12. Pour off that excess fat and stir in your flour.
13. Cook for 60 seconds.
14. Add your ketchup and then your broth.
15. Bring to a boil and then reduce your heat and simmer for 5 minutes.
16. Get a casserole dish (2 quarts).
17. Spread the beef in a layer before adding the carrots and potatoes.
18. Place your cheese on top.
19. Bake for 20 minutes. It should have a golden brown color.

Nutritional: *Calories-452, Fat-17 grams, Carbs-52.5 grams*

PREPARATION+COOK TIME: 1 H 30 M　　　**SERVES: 6**

BAKED MACARONI AND CHEESE

INGREDIENTS

- A quarter of a teaspoon of mustard (ground)
- A single tablespoon and a half of butter that has been cut into small pieces
- 2 cups of milk that is low fat
- A single pound of sharp shredded cheddar cheese
- A single package of elbow macaroni
- 2 tablespoons of flour that is all-purpose
- A quarter teaspoon of salt
- A quarter of a teaspoon of black pepper

DIRECTIONS

1. Have an oven that is preheated to 375 F.
2. Get a 9 by 13 casserole dish.
3. Stay the dish.
4. Cook the macaroni, when it's tender, drain it.
5. When the pasta is cooking, combine the 2 and a half cups of cheese with the mustard, flour, and pepper.
6. Get a bowl and combine the cheese mix you just made with the hot pasta and stir it to combine.
7. Pour into the pan.
8. Pour your milk over the pasta.
9. Top the dish with cheese.
10. Dot with butter.
11. Cover with aluminum foil.
12. Bake for 45 minutes. If you choose to, you can take the foil off at the half-hour mark.
13. It should be firm and a brownish golden color.
14. If you let it sit for 10 minutes before serving, you should be able to let it firm up further.

Nutritional: *Calories-220, Fat- 6 grams, Carbs-34 grams, Protein-10 grams, Fiber-5 grams*

PREPARATION+COOK TIME: 1 H 15 M **SERVES: 2**

LASAGNA

INGREDIENTS

- A half teaspoon of salt
- A single cup of shredded cheese (use cheddar)
- A quarter teaspoon of pepper
- A whole wheat pie crust that measures 9 inches
- ¾ of a cup of milk (use whole milk)
- 5 eggs (large)
- 2 cups of florets of broccoli

DIRECTIONS

1. Get a large skillet.
2. Put your heat to medium.
3. Brown your ground beef before draining all the grease.
4. Add the sauce and simmer for 5 minutes.
5. Get a bowl.
6. Mix mozzarella cheese (leave one cup out), eggs, cottage cheese, spices, and half of the parmesan cheese.
7. Get a baking dish that is 9 by 13.
8. Spread ¾ of the sauce mix in the pan and then place 3 lasagna noodles (uncooked) over it.
9. Then place the remaining mozzarella and parmesan cheese.
10. Add half a cup of water to your edges of the pan.
11. Cover with your aluminum foil.
12. Heat your oven to 350 F.
13. Bake for 45 minutes.
14. Uncover your dish.
15. Bake ten more minutes.
16. Let it stand for ten minutes; then it's ready.

Nutritional: *Calories-377, Fat-26.4 grams, Carbs-26.4 grams, Protein-29.4 grams*

PREPARATION+COOK TIME: 40 M   **SERVES: 1**

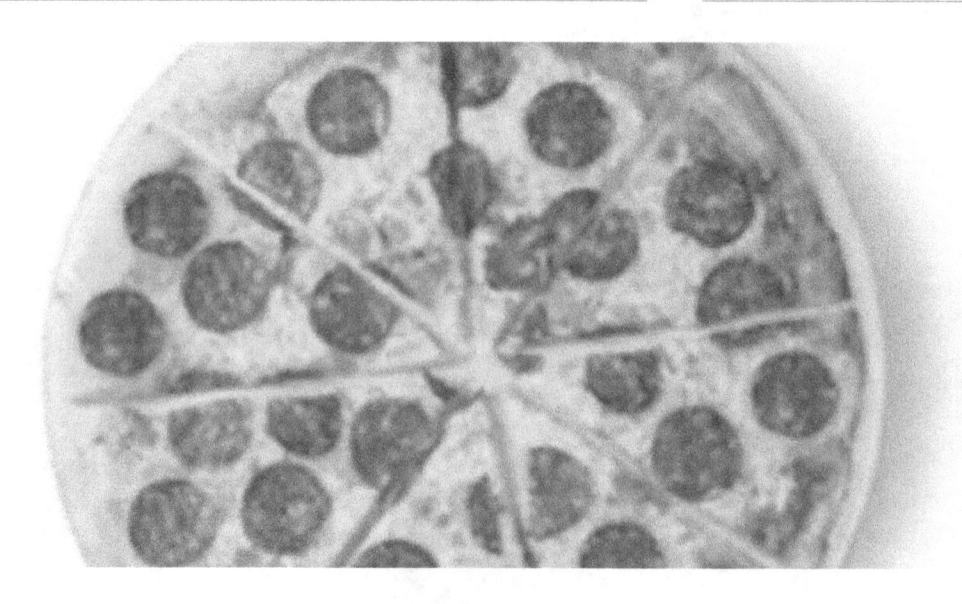

PIZZA

INGREDIENTS

- A single pound and a half of pizza dough
- A single cup of basil leaves that are torn and fresh
- 8 ounces of sliced mozzarella cheese
- 28 ounce can of tomatoes that are whole, peeled and drained
- 4 large minced garlic cloves

DIRECTIONS

1. Heat your oven to 450 degrees.
2. If you choose to use a pizza stone in the oven to warm.
3. Roll out your dough on a surface that is lightly floured.
4. Press into a large circle gently and make sure that it is a quarter-inch thick.

For the sauce:
5. Get a bowl.
6. Crush the tomatoes in the bowl.
7. Add garlic and spices (salt and pepper) in the bowl and stir it before placing it to the side.
8. Place the sauce on the dough and then add cheese and half of the basil.

Last instructions:
9. Bake for 25 minutes until the cheese is bubbling and the crust is golden in color. Place the rest of the basil on top.

Nutritional: *Calories-390, Fat-11 grams, Carbs- 52 grams, Protein-15 grams, Fiber- 3 grams*

PREPARATION+COOK TIME: 1 H 10 M **SERVES: 4**

MEATLOAF

INGREDIENTS

- Half a teaspoon of both salt and pepper (ground pepper)
- Half a cup of diced onion
- A single egg
- A single cup of grated parmesan cheese
- 16 ounces of ground beef that is 90% grass-fed and lean
- A quarter of a cup of ketchup and a third of a cup of ketchup

DIRECTIONS

1. Heat the oven to 350 F.
2. Get a loaf pan.
3. Line it with aluminum foil.
4. Dice the onion finely.
5. Mix all of your ingredients in a bowl except for the last third of a cup of ketchup. Either use your hands or something to stir it.
6. Form it into a loaf and stick it in the pan topping it with the rest of the ketchup.
7. Bake for 60 minutes.
8. When finished, let stand for 5 minutes.

Nutritional: *Calories-342, Fat-17.5 grams, Protein-36.2 grams, Carbs-9.6 grams*

PREPARATION+COOK TIME: 1 H   **SERVES: 4**

CHICKEN FIESTA BAKE

INGREDIENTS

- 2-3 chicken breasts that have been sliced widthwise in half
- Taco seasoning
- Half a cup of medium cheddar cheese
- Diced green onion
- A single 16 ounce of salsa (medium)
- A single can of undrained corn
- A cup of rice that is white and long grain
- A third of a cup of water
- A single can of drained and rinsed black beans

DIRECTIONS

1. 2-3 chicken breasts that have been sliced widthwise in half
2. Taco seasoning
3. Half a cup of medium cheddar cheese
4. Diced green onion
5. A single 16 ounce of salsa (medium)
6. A single can of undrained corn
7. A cup of rice that is white and long grain
8. A third of a cup of water
9. A single can of drained and rinsed black beans

Nutritional: *Calories-220, Fat- 6 grams, Carbs-34 grams, Protein-10 grams, Fiber-5 grams*

PREPARATION+COOK TIME: 1 H 15 M **SERVES: 4**

CHICKEN & RICE CASSEROLE

INGREDIENTS

- 4 breasts of chicken
- A cup and a half of water
- A single of white rice that is uncooked and long grain
- A single package of onion soup mix
- A single 10 ounce can of cream of mushroom soup that is condensed

DIRECTIONS

1. Heat your oven to 325 F.
2. Get a 9 by 13 pan and spray it with cooking spray.
3. Add your chicken and season it (with pepper and salt)
4. Pour the rice over the chicken. The rice should be uncooked.
5. Sprinkle with the soup mix.
6. Combine the water and the soup and pour it over the chicken.
7. Cover it and then bake it for an hour and fifteen minutes. The rice should be tender.

Nutritional: *Calories-470, Fat- 7 grams, Carbs- 40 grams, Protein- 54 grams*

CHAPTER 4:
BAKED SNACK RECIPES

PREPARATION+COOK TIME: 20 M   SERVES: 6

CHEDDAR BISCUITS

INGREDIENTS

- 2 cups of biscuit mix
- A quarter cup of butter
- ⅔ of a cup of milk
- A single cup of mild cheddar cheese that is shredded
- A quarter teaspoon of garlic powder

DIRECTIONS

1. Heat your oven to 450 F.
2. Grease a baking sheet.
3. Mix the biscuit mix, milk, and cheese in a bowl. Make sure that the batter is doughy and soft. A wooden spoon will help with this, and it should take half a minute.
4. Put the batter on the sheet in spoonfuls.
5. Bake 10 minutes, and the biscuits should be a light brown.
6. Heat the garlic and butter in a pan on low heat until it is melted. This will take 5 minutes.
7. Brush that mix over the biscuits.

Nutritional: *Calories-385, Fat-24.6 grams, Carbs-31.5 grams, Protein-10.2 grams*

PREPARATION+COOK TIME: 1 H 45 M **SERVES: 2**

ALMOND-RAISIN GRANOLA

INGREDIENTS

- Half a cup of flax seeds
- Half a cup of sunflower seed kernels
- A cup of raw almonds that are sliced
- 3 cups of oats that are old-fashioned
- A quarter cup of melted coconut oil
- A single cup of raisins
- 6 tablespoons of honey
- 6 tablespoons of pure maple syrup
- 2 tablespoons of water that is warm

DIRECTIONS

1. Heat your oven to 250 and line a jelly roll pan with baking parchment.
2. Mix everything but the water, oil, honey, and syrup in a bowl and whisk the water, oil, honey, and syrup in another bowl. Make sure that the honey mix is smooth.
3. Pour the oat mix bowl into the honey bowl.
4. Spread the mix on the pan in a layer that is even.
5. Bake for an hour but up to an hour and a half until the color is a golden brown.
6. Take out of the oven and make sure that you let it cool completely.
7. Take the granola off by lifting the paper.
8. Break it and place in a bowl adding your choice of ingredients and then mix it.
9. Store in a container that is airtight.

Nutritional: *Calories-568, Protein-12.4 grams, Fat-27.2 grams, Carbs0-76.4 grams*

PREPARATION+COOK TIME: 1 H 10 M **SERVES: 12**

BANANA BREAD

INGREDIENTS

- A single teaspoon of baking soda
- ¾ of a cup of sugar
- Half a cup of pecans that have been chopped
- 3 bananas medium in size and mashed
- Half a cup of mayonnaise
- A single egg
- A cup and a half of flour

DIRECTIONS

1. Preheat your oven to 350.
2. Get a bowl.
3. Mix the egg, mayonnaise, and bananas.
4. Get another bowl.
5. Mix the baking soda, pecans, flour, and sugar in the bowl.
6. Add the flour mix to the wet mix and stir until combined.
7. The mix will be very thick; this is alright. If you over-mix, it won't be right.
8. Grease a pan.
9. Pour the mix into the pan and bake for an hour. A toothpick should come out clean.
10. Remove from the pan and make sure it cools completely.

Nutritional: *Calories-231, Fat-10 grams, Fiber- 1 gram, Protein-2 grams, Carbs-31 grams*

PREPARATION+COOK TIME: 1 H   **SERVES: 12**

CROISSANTS

INGREDIENTS

- A single cup of milk
- 4 cups of flour that is all-purpose
- A third of a cup of sugar that is granulated
- 2 and a quarter teaspoons of salt that is kosher
- 4 teaspoons of yeast that is active and dry
- A cup and a quarter of butter that is cold and unsalted
- An egg wash (this is to have a single large egg, and you beat it with a teaspoon of water)

DIRECTIONS

1. Place your yeast and salt along with the flour and sugar in a bowl and whisk it all together until it has combined well.
2. Slice your butter into slices an eighth of an inch thick and toss it into the flour mix so that the butter is coated.
3. Add your milk in and stir it together. A stiff dough will be made.
4. Wrap your dough and make sure it's tight. You are going to use plastic wrap. Let it chill for 60 minutes.
5. Get yourself a lightly floured surface and roll your dough into a big and long rectangle.
6. Fold and make it like a letter. This means you fold it into thirds. Turn it 90 degrees and repeat 4 times.
7. The dough should be flat and smooth with streaks of butter in it.
8. Rewrap it again and chill for another 60 minutes. Divide the dough in half and then roll again.
9. It should be an eighth of an inch thick.
10. Cut your dough into triangles that are long and skinny.
11. Notch your wide end of each triangle you made with a half-inch cut.
12. Roll from the wide end to the end with a point. Tuck the point under the croissant.
13. Place on a baking sheet that is lined with parchment.
14. Cover with plastic wrap (loosely) and allow it to proof for 120 minutes.
15. Preheat your oven to 375 F.
16. Brush the croissants with your egg wash.
17. Bake 20 minutes.
18. They should be a puffy brown golden color, and they should be flaky.

Nutritional: *Calories-294, Fat-16 grams, Protein- 5 grams, Fiber- 1 gram, Carbs-31 grams*

PREPARATION+COOK TIME: 2 H 20 M **SERVES: 12**

JAM POCKETS

INGREDIENTS

- A single teaspoon of vanilla
- A single egg
- 2 cups of flour
- Half a cup of powdered sugar
- A single cup of butter that is cut into cubes and cold

DIRECTIONS

1. Preheat your oven to 375.
2. Use a food processor and combine your sugar and flour until they have mixed.
3. Toss in your butter and give it a few long buzzes with it until it has a cornmeal look.
4. Add the vanilla and egg and then buzz it twice more. You should be left with a soft dough.
5. Cover with plastic wrap and then let it chill in the fridge for a couple of hours.
6. Roll out our dough and use a cookie cutter to make circles.
7. Add the jam of your choice to the center and fold your edges inward. It should overlap in the middle.
8. Bake 10 minutes.
9. The bottom should be a faint brown color.
10. When cooled, sprinkle sugar over the top.

Nutritional: *Calories-220, Fat- 6 grams, Carbs-34 grams, Protein-10 grams, Fiber-5 grams*

PREPARATION+COOK TIME: 40 M **SERVES: 4**

PIZZA POCKETS

INGREDIENTS

- A third of a cup of Parmesan that is grated
- A quarter of a cup of Parmesan that is grated
- 8 ounces of turkey sausage (Italian)
- A single tablespoon of olive oil
- A single beaten egg
- A single cup and a half of marinara sauce
- All-purpose flour
- A single pizza crust store-bought
- 4 ounces of room temperature cream cheese
- A cup of arugula tightly packed

DIRECTIONS

1. Heat your olive oil over a heat that is medium-high and in a medium heavy skillet.
2. Add in the sausage and cook until it is golden and crumbled. 5 minutes.
3. Add the arugula and cook it until it has wilted.
4. Turn off your heat and let it cool for 19 minutes.
5. Add in your cream cheese and a third of the parmesan.
6. Stir, so it combines.
7. Set it aside.
8. Preheat your oven to 400 F.
9. Roll out your dough and make a big rectangle.
10. Cut it in half.
11. Do this again until you have eight equal rectangles.
12. Put your toppings onto one of the sides of each rectangle.
13. Brush the edges with egg wash.
14. Close the rectangle of dough over the topping.
15. Use a fork to seal them up.
16. Put the pockets on the baking sheet that is lined with parchment paper.
17. Brush the tops with egg wash.
18. Sprinkle the rest of the cheese on top.
19. Bake for 15 minutes.
20. Heat your marinara sauce over a low heat.
21. Serve with sauce when done.

Nutritional: *Calories-385, Fat- 19 grams, Carbs-37 grams, Protein-17 grams, Fiber-1.5 grams*

PREPARATION+COOK TIME: 30 M **SERVES: 10**

SMOKY PRETZEL MIX

INGREDIENTS

- A single cup of almonds that are smoked
- A single cup of mini pretzels
- 2 teaspoons of chipotle chili powder
- A single teaspoon of paprika that is smoked
- 2 cups corn snack crackers
- 2 cups of rice cereal squares
- 2 cups of white cheddar cheese crackers in bite-size
- 6 tablespoons of butter that is unsalted

DIRECTIONS

1. Heat the oven to 325.
2. Toss everything together except the butter and spices in a bowl.
3. Melt the butter in a pan over medium heat.
4. Stir in chili powder, paprika, and garlic.
5. Drizzle over the mix.
6. Toss to coat evenly.
7. Spread it on a rimmed baking sheet that you lined with parchment paper.
8. Bake for 12 minutes. Stir once during this time.
9. Cool totally on the sheet.
10. Store in a container that is airtight.

Nutritional: *Calories-220, Fat- 6 grams, Carbs-34 grams, Protein-10 grams, Fiber-5 grams*

PREPARATION+COOK TIME: 1 H 30 M **SERVES: 6**

BLUEBERRY POUND CAKE

INGREDIENTS

- 2 Tablespoons of butter
- A quarter cup of white sugar
- 2 ¾ cups of all-purpose flour
- A single teaspoon of baking powder
- A single cup of butter
- 4 eggs
- 2 cups of white sugar
- 2 cups of blueberries that are fresh
- A single teaspoon of vanilla extract
- A quarter cup of flour that is all-purpose

DIRECTIONS

1. Preheat your oven to 325 F.
2. Grease a pan that is 10 inches with 2 tablespoons of butter.
3. Sprinkle that same pan with a quarter cup of sugar.
4. Mix 2 ¾ of the cup of flour with the baking powder and place it to the side.
5. Get a bowl and cream a cup of butter and 2 cups of sugar together until it has become fluffy and light.
6. Beat the eggs one at a time before stirring the vanilla in.
7. Slowly beat in your flour mix.
8. Dredge your berries with the last quarter cup of flour.
9. Fold into the batter before pouring it in your prepared pan.
10. Bake for 80 minutes. The toothpick test should show a clean toothpick.
11. Let cool for 10 minutes into the pan before letting it totally cool on a wire rack.

Nutritional: *Calories-338, Fat-14.5 grams, Carbs-48.8 grams, Protein-4.3 grams*

PREPARATION+COOK TIME: 1 H 10 M **SERVES: 12**

ZUCCHINI BREAD

INGREDIENTS

- Half a teaspoon of baking powder
- Half a teaspoon of all-purpose flour
- Half a teaspoon of baking soda
- Half a teaspoon of ground cinnamon
- Half a cup of unsweetened applesauce
- A single cup and a half of zucchini that has been lightly packed but not drained of liquid and grated
- A single cup of granulated sugar
- A quarter cup of packed brown sugar (light)
- 2 eggs (large)
- A single teaspoon of vanilla extract
- A third of a cup of vegetable oil

DIRECTIONS

1. Heat your oven to 350 F.
2. Get a 9 by 5 loaf pan and spray it with cooking spray.
3. Get a bowl and add everything in but the baking powder, flour, and cinnamon along with the baking soda.
4. Whisk all of these together until they have combined well.
5. Add in the cinnamon and baking soda along with the flour and baking powder and stir until there is no dry flour remains. Do not over mix this, however.
6. Pour the batter in the pan and bake for 50 minutes. A toothpick should have moist crumbs on it.
7. Cool for 10 minutes.
8. Move to a cooling rack and let it cool totally.

Nutritional: *Calories-213, Carbs-35 grams, Protein-3 grams, Fat- 7 grams*

PREPARATION+COOK TIME: 1 H   **SERVES: 12**

LEMON RASPBERRY MUFFINS

INGREDIENTS

- Half a cup of honey
- 2 eggs
- A single cup of plain Greek yogurt
- A single cup and ¾ of white whole wheat flour
- A single teaspoon of baking powder
- Half a teaspoon of baking soda
- A third of a cup of coconut oil that is melted
- 2 teaspoons of vanilla extract
- The zest from a lemon
- A single cup and a half of organic raspberries
- A single tablespoon of turbinado sugar

DIRECTIONS

1. Heat your oven to 350 F.
2. Grease a 12 cup muffin tin with coconut oil or cooking spray.
3. Get a large bowl.
4. Combine flour, baking soda, baking powder, and blend together with a whisk.
5. Get another bowl and combine the honey oil, and beat them together with a whisk.
6. Add in the eggs and beat them well before adding the zest, vanilla, and yogurt.
7. Mix it all well. If the oil gets solid, microwave it for half a minute.
8. Pour your wet ingredients into the dry.
9. Mix it with a large spoon until it has just combined.
10. Fold raspberries in the batter. It will be thick.
11. Divided into the 12 cups and add sugar to the top.
12. Bake 24 minutes and toothpick should come out clean.
13. Let cool on a cooling rack.

Nutritional: *Calories-193, Fat-7.5 grams, Carbs-28.7 grams, Protein-5.3 grams*

CHAPTER 5:
BAKED DESSERT RECIPES

PREPARATION+COOK TIME: 1 H **SERVES: 6**

CHOCOLATE CAKE

INGREDIENTS

- 2 cups of white sugar
- A cup and a 3/4 of flour that is all-purpose
- 2 eggs
- A single cup of milk
- Half a cup of vegetable oil
- ¾ of a cup of cocoa powder that has been unsweetened
- A single teaspoon and a half of baking powder
- A single teaspoon and a half of baking soda
- 2 teaspoons of vanilla extract
- A single cup of water that is boiling

DIRECTIONS

1. Heat the oven to 350 F.
2. Grease and flour 2 round pans that are 9 inches.
3. Get a bowl.
4. Mix everything in a bowl but the eggs, vanilla, and oil. Don't use the water yet either.
5. Stir everything together.
6. Add the oil, vanilla, and eggs, and the milk and mix for 2 minutes with a mixer on medium speed.
7. Stir in the water.
8. Pour in the pans.
9. Bake for a half-hour.
10. Cool for 10 minutes before you move to a wire rack.

Nutritional: *Calories-157, Fat-5.7 grams, Carbs-25.7 grams, Protein-2.3 grams*

PREPARATION+COOK TIME: 2 H   **SERVES: 2**

CARROT CAKE

INGREDIENTS

- 2 teaspoons of cinnamon that is ground
- 2 cups of flour that is all-purpose
- 2 cups of white sugar
- 4 eggs
- A single cup and a quarter of vegetable oil
- 2 teaspoons of extract of vanilla
- 2 teaspoons of baking soda
- 2 teaspoons of baking powder
- 3 cups of carrots that are grated
- A single cup of pecans that are chopped
- Half a cup of softened butter
- A teaspoon of extract of vanilla
- 4 cups of confectioner's sugar
- 8 ounces of softened cream cheese
- A single cup of pecans that are chopped

DIRECTIONS

1. Heat your oven to 350.
2. Get a bowl and set it aside before you get a pan that is 9 by 13 and you grease and flour it.
3. Beat your eggs, vanilla, sugar, and oil together.
4. Mix in the baking powder and soda along with your cinnamon and flour.
5. Then stir in the carrots before you fold in your pecans.
6. Pour the mix in the pan that you prepared for the oven.
7. Bake for 50 minutes and then let cool for ten before you move it to a wire rack.
8. Let cool totally.

For the topping:

9. Get a bowl and combine everything before beating it. When it's creamy, add in the pecans that are chopped.
10. Put it on top.

Nutritional: *Calories-575, Fat-34.8, Carbs-63.7 grams*

PREPARATION+COOK TIME: 1 H 30 M　　　　**SERVES: 6**

CHEESECAKE

INGREDIENTS

- A single cup of sour cream
- 2 Teaspoons of vanilla
- 3 eggs
- 3 (8 ounces) packages of softened cream cheese
- A third of a cup of divided sugar
- A third of a cup of melted butter
- A cup and ¾ of graham cracker crumbs
- A single can of cherry pie filling (go for 21 ounces

DIRECTIONS

1. Heat your oven to 350.
2. Mix the crumbs, sugar and butter and press into a springform pan that is 9 inches.
3. Beat the cream cheese and leftover sugar using a mixer.
4. Mix until it is blended.
5. Add vanilla and sour cream, and make sure to mix it all well before adding in your egg. Go one at a time and beat it all on low speed.
6. Pour it over the crust.
7. Bake for 60 minutes.
8. You can top it with the filling.

Nutritional: *Calories-313, Fat-17.7 grams, Carbs-35.8 grams*

PREPARATION+COOK TIME: 1 H **SERVES: 6**

BROWNIES

INGREDIENTS

- A third of a cup of cocoa powder that is unsweetened
- Half a cup of all-purpose flour
- 2 eggs
- A single cup of white sugar
- Half a cup of butter
- A single teaspoon of vanilla extract
- A quarter of a teaspoon of baking powder

The icing
- A single tablespoon of honey
- A single teaspoon of vanilla extract
- A single cup of confectioners sugar
- 3 tablespoons of softened butter
- 3 tablespoon of cocoa powder that is unsweetened

DIRECTIONS

1. Preheat your oven to 350.
2. Get a pan and melt the butter.
3. Take it away from the heat and add in the sugar, egg, and vanilla.
4. Stir it and then beat in the flour,cocoa and baking powder.
5. Spread in a pan that is prepared.
6. Bake a half hour.

For the icing:
7. Combine everything and stir it.
8. Put it on the brownie.

Nutritional: Calories-183, Fat-9 grams, Carbs-25.7 grams

PREPARATION+COOK TIME: 1 H **SERVES: 15**

BLONDIES

INGREDIENTS

- A single cup of melted and unsalted butter
- 2 and a half cups of flour that is all-purpose
- 2 large eggs and a single egg yolk
- A cup and a quarter of brown sugar that has been tightly packed
- Half a cup of sugar
- 2 teaspoons of vanilla extract
- A single cup of walnuts that are chopped
- ⅔ of a cup of white chocolate chips
- Half of a teaspoon of baking powder
- 2 teaspoons of cornstarch

DIRECTIONS

1. Preheat your oven to 350 F.
2. Line a 13 by 9 pan with parchment paper.
3. Combine your sugar and melted butter in a bowl.
4. Add your yolk, eggs, and vanilla extract and then stir until everything has been fully combined.
5. Set this to the side.
6. In another bowl, whisk your other ingredients together except the nuts and chocolate chips.
7. Then fold the nuts and chips in.
8. Put the batter in the pan.
9. Put it in the oven and bake for a half-hour.
10. Let cool.

Nutritional: *Calories-370, Fat-20 grams, Carbs-46 grams, Protein-4 grams*

PREPARATION+COOK TIME: 1 H **SERVES: 6**

CHOCOLATE CHIP COOKIES

INGREDIENTS

- A single cup of softened butter
- 2 eggs
- 2 teaspoons of vanilla extract
- A single teaspoon of baking soda
- A single cup of white sugar
- A single cup of brown sugar that is packed
- 2 cups of chocolate chips that are semi-sweet
- 3 cups of all-purpose flour
- A single cup of walnuts that are chopped
- 2 teaspoons of hot water

DIRECTIONS

1. Heat the oven to 350 F.
2. Cream together the sugar and butter until it's smooth.
3. Beat in your eggs one at a time and stir in your vanilla.
4. Dissolve the baking soda in your hot water.
5. Add in the butter before stirring in the nuts and chips.
6. Drop spoonfuls onto a pan.
7. Bake １o minutes.

Nutritional: *Calories-298, Fat-15.6 grams, Carbs-38.8 grams, Protein-3.6 grams*

PREPARATION+COOK TIME: 1 H **SERVES: 6**

SNICKERDOODLES

INGREDIENTS

- 2 eggs
- Half of a cup of shortening
- A half of a cup of softened butter
- A cup and a half of white sugar
- 2 teaspoons of cinnamon that is ground
- 2 tablespoons of white sugar
- 2 teaspoons of extract of vanilla
- A single teaspoon of baking soda
- 2 teaspoons of tartar (cream of tartar)
- 2 ¾ cups of flour that is all-purpose

DIRECTIONS

1. Heat up your 400 F.
2. Cream the butter, sugar, eggs, vanilla, and shortening before blending in tartar, soda, and flour.
3. Shape your dough and put it into balls.
4. Mix up your sugar (the tablespoons) and cinnamon.
5. Roll your dough in that mix.
6. Bake 10 minutes.
7. Remove right away from the baking sheets.

Nutritional: *Calories-92, Fat-4.3 gram, Carbs-12.4 grams*

PREPARATION+COOK TIME: 1 H 20 M　　　**SERVES: 8**

APPLE PIE

INGREDIENTS

- A quarter teaspoon of ground ginger
- Half a cup of sugar
- Half a cup of brown sugar that is packed
- A single teaspoon of cinnamon that is ground
- 3 tablespoons of flour that is all-purpose
- A single tablespoon of lemon juice from a lemon
- A single tablespoon of butter
- A single, double-crust pie
- Half a dozen tart apples that are sliced thinly
- A single white large egg
- A quarter teaspoon of nutmeg that is ground

DIRECTIONS

1. Get a bowl and combine the spices, flour, and sugars.
2. In another bowl, put in the lemon juice and toss the apples in it.
3. Add in the sugar mix and toss so they are coated.
4. Line the pie plate with bottom crust and trim so that it is even with the edge.
5. Fill it with the apple mix and dot with butter.
6. Roll the rest of the crust on top to fit the top.
7. Place it over the filling.
8. Trim before sealing and fluting the edges.
9. Cut slits into the crust.
10. Beat the egg white until it becomes foamy and brush it over that crust.
11. Place sugar over it.
12. Cover those edges with foil but do it loosely.
13. Bake for 25 minutes at a heat of 375.
14. Take off the foil and bake until the crust is a golden brown color and the filling is nice and bubbly.
15. This will take an additional 25 minutes.
16. Let it cool on a wire rack.

Nutritional: *Calories-414, Fat-16 grams, Carbs-67 grams*

PREPARATION+COOK TIME: 1 H 5 M   **SERVES: 12**

COFFEE CAKE

INGREDIENTS

For your topping:
- A single cup of flour that is all-purpose
- A single tablespoon and a half of cinnamon that is ground
- A single cup of brown sugar that is light
- Half a dozen tablespoons of melted butter

For the cake itself:
- A single cup of sugar that is granulated
- A single cup of room temperature butter
- 3/4 of a cup of sour cream
- 3 teaspoons of baking powder
- ⅔ of a cup of brown sugar that is light

DIRECTIONS

1. Make sure that your oven is heated to 350 F.
2. Get a 9 by 13 baking dish and spray with nonstick spray.
3. Place to the side.
4. Get a bowl and whisk together the items for the filling before putting it to the side as well.
5. For the topping mix everything together in a bowl, and it should look like crumbs. Form pieces with your hands. Place to the side.
6. As for the cake, mix your sugar and butter in a bowl and use a mixer at medium speed for 120 seconds.
7. It should be fluffy and light.
8. You need to add in the sour cream, vanilla, eggs, and baking powder and mix for 60 seconds. It should be combined, and it should be smooth as well.
9. Put your mixer to a low setting and add in the milk and flour (alternating the portions) begin with the flour, end with the flour.
10. Mix until it is smooth and just combined.

INGREDIENTS

- 3 eggs
- A single tablespoon of vanilla extract
- A single cup and a quarter of milk
- 3 ⅔ cup of flour that is all-purpose

For the filling:
- ¾ of a cup of flour that is all-purpose
- 2 teaspoons of cinnamon that is ground
- ¾ of a cup of brown sugar that is light

For the icing:
- 2-3 tablespoons of milk
- A single cup of powdered sugar

DIRECTIONS

11. Spread half of the batter in the pan and sprinkle the filling over the top. Then place the remaining batter on top.
12. Place the topping on top.
13. Bake for 45 minutes.
14. Remove from the oven and place on a wire rack.
15. Let it totally cool.
16. Drizzle the icing on top.

Nutritional: *Calories-660, Fat-24.9 grams, Carbs-101.1 grams, Protein-9.6 grams*

PREPARATION+COOK TIME: 1 H 30 M   **SERVES: 6**

LEMON BARS

INGREDIENTS

- A single cup of softened butter
- A single cup and a half of white sugar
- A quarter cup of all-purpose flour
- Half a cup of white sugar
- 2 juiced lemons

DIRECTIONS

1. Heat your oven to 350 F.
2. Get a bowl.
3. Blend half a cup of sugar and 2 cups of flour along with butter that has softened.
4. Get a 9 by 13 pan and press it into the bottom.
5. Bake 20 minutes.
6. Get a bowl.
7. Whisk a quarter cup of flour and a cup and a half of a cup of sugar.
8. Whisk in the lemon juice and the eggs.
9. Pour over the crust.
10. Bake another 20 minutes.
11. They will firm as they cool.

Nutritional: Calories-126, Fat-5.8 grams, Carbs-17.8 grams, Protein-1.6 grams

CHAPTER 6: IDEAS FOR MORE BAKING FUN

Baking is a really fun thing to do not just like yourself while you're trying to grow your skills and learn how to cook and bake properly to become the best chef that you can be, it's also a really great way to open up your creativity and have fun with your family. Baking has long since been a family tradition, and it's a great way to learn some quality time in the kitchen as well. It brings families together and friends together and can create a great sense of community. All it takes is a couple of recipes, some ingredients and to know what it is that you want to make or an idea that you want to try.

It's also a lot more satisfying than being stuck on social media for five hours. This is a trap that many fall into. You already know what celebrities are doing and what fashion is trending right now. As such, you don't need to spend half a day on Instagram. Instead, why not makes an irresistible dish in the kitchen and your skills to become better and make better food? Some great things that you can make and some great ideas for more baking fun are to try making some of the following items for yourself.

- **Banana scones**-you can make them vegan or gluten-free, depending on what you put in them.

- **A giant brownie**

- You can make pull-apart cinnamon rolls as well. The reason that we mentioned these though we've already had a recipe above is because there are literally hundreds of different ways to do a cinnamon roll and each one is unique to the baker.

- Donuts. You don't have to go traditional here. You can make donuts which are different than other donuts that you see every day. Instead of making chocolate or vanilla or something that's everywhere else that you go, you could try making a cream cheese donut or an herb encrusted donut instead.

- Chocolate chip cupcakes with avocado icing or strawberry icing instead of the typical vanilla icing.

You can honestly make just about anything as long as you're creative. Everyone is also looking for great ways to be healthy, so instead of just making sweet and decadent desserts, you could also try these ideas for people who are more healthy options. If you are one of those or wish to cook for them, try these.

- Baked fruit-there are many different ways that you can do this, and there are literally thousands of ingredients that you can use for these recipes.

- You can make baked apples with nuts, or you can bake peaches as well.

- In addition to this, you can make grapefruit and pineapple, mangos and many other fruits that would taste amazing in a baked dish.

- Another example of this is scones. Scones are a great British dish, and you can make them with dark chocolate or oranges, you can make them with strawberries, blueberries, there are a lot of healthy ingredients that you can use that would make this a great dessert.

- Another great idea is to do something like a cheesecake that has hundreds of different variations as well.

Following unique trends can be fun as well, and a great example here would be the Funfetti cupcakes. These are cupcakes that are Instagram worthy and are covered with different sprinkles and flavors. You could also turn the salty dish into a sweet dish by making chocolate chip stuffed pretzels or making chocolate covered pretzels. Turning salty into sweet can be really fun and turning salty or sweet and savory can take some real creativity and talent.

For a new popular idea, you could try to begin making banana bread, but you could also put a twist on this as well. Instead of just making regular banana bread, you can make blueberry banana bread, strawberry banana bread, raisin bread or get really innovative and try something like papaya bread or mango bread for a new twist. If you like tiramisu, you could make something new and different like tiramisu cupcakes instead of just regular cupcakes or regular tiramisu. This adds a twist that lets them see how creative you really are. When you're baking the options are endless, it just depends on your own creativity. You can use your imagination to take you to the limit or find that your mind and passion have no limit.

nother example is that if it's fall, you can make cookies in the shapes of leaves. By that same token, if it's winter, you can make snowflakes. On somebody's birthday, you could bake a cake in numbers or letters, so you can have baking ideas that are based on your favorite movies if you like such as Disney or Paw Patrol for a child's birthday party. You can make cupcakes or cookies look like the characters from their favorite movies and this would bring a massive delight to the people around you. Another good example is if it's Halloween, you could bake monster cookies with little eyes or Dracula cookies with little fangs.

Take holidays and ideas from other cultures as well. If it's Cinco de Mayo or another holiday that is cultural, you can learn about their culture and see what would be appropriate and fun to make. If you find that you are getting bored following trends is also another great way to keep your creativity flowing. For example, unicorn cake is a very popular dish as well right now, and it's because everybody has uncovered their obsession with unicorns and Instagram. Everyone wants to take beautiful pictures and show everybody what they can do and this is something that you can do too and make your own wonderful creations. This wouldn't be the main goal here of course, but it is a great example of showing how social media does play a part in what you can make because it will give you fresh ideas. The trick here is not to get stuck on it so that you're so focused on it instead of other things like those ideas and the dishes that you want to make for yourself.

CHAPTER 7: BAKING IDEAS TO DO TOGETHER

In this chapter, we will be giving you a few ideas on baking that you can do together. If you want to bake as a family, a great thing that you can learn how to do is desserts. You can also help with other meals as well. Breakfast, lunch, dinner, and snacks are all things that you can help them with too or they can help you. These are all important parts of the day and they all give you different nutritional values as well as playing a different structural part in your day. As a chef, you need to know which meal is going to give you the most benefit and what is going to make the people around you happy. When you are a chef you're not just cooking for yourself but you're cooking for the people around you and you want them to have a wonderful experience with your food. You want them to be able to feel what you're feeling with your dishes and you want them to be able to feel your passion and creativity. When you are baking, it can be a lovely experience that makes you happy and feels great about yourself.

There are many different ways that you can have fun and bake together, and the first thing that you need to do in order to achieve this is you could all go shopping together for the ingredients. That is where the baking starts and you can't bake without the proper tools. You could work on the recipe together and begin to start the process together as well. Just being together in the kitchen will give you a sense of camaraderie as a family and it will bring you closer together with the people you care about. Cooking and baking is a great way to bond and you hear many stories from grandparents and mothers about how they used to bake cakes and pies around the holidays with their families or their loved ones. This is something that you can do too and it's a great way to have more fun baking together.

There's also a lot of different recipes that you can try when you're just starting out. Many people start out with deserts because they have a sweet tooth or vanilla-like food that is considered to be junk food but in keeping our bodies as healthy as possible, there's also a lot of new ingredients that you can use as well that are found in health food such as fruits and vegetables. You can bake with all of these ingredients as well which is a great idea for when you're trying to learn how to do this together and have fun. One of the great things about this if you want to do this as a family is to assign jobs to everybody. Have one person read through the ingredients, have the other person read the recipe as well. You could have one person be the cleaning person, one person watching the oven and helping with making sure that everything is going all right, but the best part is you can all taste the dish as you're making it. This is a great way to work as a team and bake together.

You can work on the recipes together and make sure that the food is being prepared in the proper way, and then at the end of the day, you have something that you've created together and it's something that's beautiful. This is ultimately what brings the family together. Making memories together and having fun making these dishes. It is what makes people want to bake. Some great ideas for baking together and recipes that would be easy to try while you're still learning are the following:

- Fruity cream cake
- hocolate chip cookie bars
- Peach cake with a mango drizzle
- monkey bread (which is a popular southern staple)
- biscuits
- cobbler
- coffee cake
- individual mixed berry cake
- crumb bars
- granola bars
- cookies such as Funfetti or peanut butter
- pie
- brownies

You could try casseroles like macaroni and other pasta dishes as well. Many pasta dishes are actually baked in the oven, which surprises people but it's not always about making things on a stove. Casseroles are a big thing in today's society and there are literally thousands of different variations of casseroles that you can make. You can also bake meats and other dishes like the following:

- Green bean casserole
- Sweet potatoes
- chicken
- Turkey
- Ham

It's literally an endless opportunity to be together as a family, which will create a more fun environment that you want to keep baking in.

"KID CHEF BAKING" CONCLUSION

Thank you for making it through to the end of *Kid Chef: Young Chef Cookbook - The Complete Baking Book for Kids Who Love to Bake and Eat*, let's hope it was informative and able to provide you with all of the tools you need to achieve your goals whatever they may be.

The next step is to try each of the recipes in this book and test your baking skills. You will want to make sure that you try lots of new things in the kitchen to discover new flavors, new recipes, new foods, and to push the boundaries of what you know.

Baking is such a great passion for having and there are so many resources out there for you to use. Always look out for new skills that you can learn to make your time in the kitchen more fun and more rewarding.

EXTRA RECIPES

PREPARATION: 10 M **DIFFICULTY: LOW** **COOKING TIME: 20 M**

CINDERELLA OMELETTE - BREAKFAST

INGREDIENTS

- 10 oz. of pumpkin
- 2 eggs
- 1 handful of grated Parmesan
- Parsley
- 1 tbsp. milk
- Salt
- Butter to taste

DIRECTIONS

1. Remove the peel and seeds from the pumpkin and cut it into cubes.
2. Put it in the oven at 180° for 10 minutes until it is soft.
3. Blend it with the blender.
4. In a bowl beat the eggs, cheese, milk, parsley and a pinch of salt with a fork (do not overdo it because the Parmesan is already tasty enough).
5. Heat a knob of butter in a pan and pour the mixture. Let the omelette thicken and then turn it to the other side.

Tips: you can add any type of vegetables such as zucchini or carrots.

PREPARATION: 20 M   **DIFFICULTY: MEDIUM**   **COOKING TIME: 15 M**

ITALIAN TIGELLA - MAIN COURSE

INGREDIENTS

- 12 oz. of flour 00
- 5 oz. of flour Manitoba
- ½ cup of water
- 5 tbsp. of milk
- 1 tbsp. of extra virgin olive oil
- 1/25 oz. of fresh brewer's yeast
- 1 pinch of salt
- A half teaspoon of sugar

DIRECTIONS

1. Put a part of the warm milk, the crumbled yeast and the sugar in a small bowl.
2. Cover and let stand for 5 minutes until a foam is formed.
3. Put the two flours in a bowl and make a hole in the center where you will put the water, the rest of the milk, the yeast, the oil
4. Gradually start to put all the rest of the water, mixing first with a spoon and then kneading with your hands.
5. Add the salt last and continue to knead for a few minutes until you get a smooth, homogeneous and very soft dough.
6. Put it in a bowl greased with oil, also grease the oil mixture, cover with plastic wrap and let it rest for about 2 hours.
7. Take the dough again without kneading it again and put it on a floured surface.
8. Divide it into 10 balls and roll them up until reaching a thickness of about 0,4 inches
9. Heat a non-stick pan and cook the tigelle one at a time over low heat otherwise, they will burn on the surface and remain raw inside.
10. You will see bubbles start to form on the surface. After a few minutes, turn them to the other side and cook them for about 10 more minutes.

Tips:they keep well until the next day closed in a plastic bag and to have them good again you can heat them again in a pan. If you want the most leavened tigelle and you have time you can rest the pasta overnight in the fridge covered with a transparent film.

PREPARATION: 5 M **DIFFICULTY: LOW** **COOKING TIME: 15 M**

YELLOW RICE - MAIN COURSE

INGREDIENTS

- 2 handfuls of rice (about 2 oz.)
- 1 oz. of soft cheese
- Grated Parmesan cheese to taste
- 1 saffron sachet
- Milk to taste

DIRECTIONS

1. Put the rice in a saucepan with high sides and cover it for a finger and a half of water.
2. Leave to cook until the rice is soft without turning it, if the water is insufficient you can add it but it must be boiling otherwise it will stop cooking the rice.
3. When cooked, add the saffron sachet, the soft cheese, the parmesan and stir well.
4. Add enough cold milk to give the right creaminess and to ensure that when it cools down it does not become too hard and dry. The milk will also serve to cool the rice to the right point.

Tips: if you want to color the rice of some other color you can add a few tablespoons of vegetable puree and it will become orange (with tomato) green (with zucchini) and you will also be able to make him eat the vegetables without them noticing. If it advances, you can put it in a non-stick pan by squeezing it well on one side and the other until a fantastic crust is created ... it is even better.

PREPARATION: 10 M   **DIFFICULTY: MEDIUM**   **COOKING TIME: 15 M**

RED RICE "PIZZA TASTE" - MAIN COURSE

INGREDIENTS

- 2 Cup of rice
- 2 cup of tomato sauce
- ½ cup of water
- 4 Oz of Mozzarella cheese
- 2 oz. of butter
- 1 teaspoon of homemade vegetable nut
- 2 tbsp. of extra virgin olive oil
- Parmesan Cheese to taste
- Basil

DIRECTIONS

1. Dissolve the teaspoon of homemade vegetable nut in warm water.
2. Put the oil in a saucepan and heat it well. When the oil is hot, put the rice and toast it for a few minutes until it becomes transparent.
3. Deglaze with the homemade nut broth and add the tomato sauce together with the basil.
4. Lower the heat and cook the rice for about 10/15 minutes until the rice is cooked.
5. Turn off the heat, add the diced mozzarella, the butter and the grated Parmesan and mix.

Tips: let the rice rest for a few minutes and, only if necessary, add a little water or broth to make it creamier. You can replace the homemade vegetable nut with salt and the butter with a spoonful of soft cream cheese. If it advances, you can put it in a baking tin sprinkled with grated Parmesan and cook it in a preheated oven at 200° for about 10 minutes.

PREPARATION: 10 M	DIFFICULTY: LOW	COOKING TIME: 20 M

COLORED MASHED POTATO - MAIN COURSE

INGREDIENTS

- 5 large potatoes
- 1 courgette
- 1 aubergine
- 1 carrot
- 1 tomato or 3 tablespoons of tomato sauce
- 1 cup of milk
- 2 oz. of butter
- Salt

DIRECTIONS

1. Put the carrot, courgette, tomato and aubergine in a saucepan with water and boil them for 10 minutes.
2. In the meantime, put the potatoes in abundant cold water on the fire, bring to a boil and cook until soft.
3. Mash the hot potatoes with the potato masher, put half the milk with the butter and salt in a saucepan
4. When it starts to boil add the mashed potatoes and mix vigorously with a whisk, add the rest of the milk.
5. Blend the courgette, carrot, tomato and aubergine with a blender in separate bowls.
6. Divide the mashed potato into 5 bowls. Leave one neutral in the others, add the carrot in one, the courgette, the aubergine in one and the tomato in the last.
7. Mix so as to make the color of each bowl of puree homogeneous and add salt if necessary.

Tips: I like the very full-bodied but if you prefer more liquid just increase the amount of milk. You can enrich the pure with grated Parmesan or you can prepare the pink puree with ham instead of with vegetables! Always crush the hot potatoes and never blend them otherwise it would become sticky.

PREPARATION: 15 M **DIFFICULTY: LOW** **COOKING TIME: 15 M**

DIFFERENT STUFFED SANDWICH - SNACK

INGREDIENTS

- 1 baguette
- 7 oz. of sliced ham
- 2 tablespoons of grated parmesan
- 4 oz. of ricotta cheese
- 1 pinch of salt
- 2 eggs

DIRECTIONS

1. Put the eggs in a bowl with a pinch of salt and the grated Parmesan and beat them with a fork.
2. Put a spoonful of oil in a pan and when it is hot put the eggs.
3. Cook the omelette on both sides for a couple of minutes and leave to cool.
4. Put half of the cooked ham in a bowl together with the ricotta cheese and pass them with the blender until you get a homogeneous cream.
5. Cut the baguette into two equal parts and with the help of a long blade knife empty it from the crumb (you can keep it aside to prepare meatballs)
6. Put the omelette on a plate and spread it with ricotta and ham mousse, put a slice of cooked ham on top and roll it tightly.
7. Place the omelette roll inside the baguette to get to the bottom.
8. When it is time to eat it you can taste it in bites like a sandwich or cut it into slices and give each one to each guest.

Tips: I gave you an idea for the filling, of course you can stuff it as you like, with tuna, ham and sliced cheese or grilled vegetables.

PREPARATION: 10 M   **DIFFICULTY: LOW**   **COOKING TIME: 10 M**

VEGETABLES STICKS - SNACK

INGREDIENTS

- 1 potato
- 1 carrot
- 2 oz. of sweet corn
- 1 courgette
- 1 generous handful of grated Parmesan
- Flour 00
- Bread crumbs
- Corn flour
- 2 eggs
- Extra virgin olive oil

DIRECTIONS

1. Boil the potato, carrot and courgette.
2. Pass them in the potato masher together with the sweet corn. It must become a fairly homogeneous compound.
3. Let it cool and add the grated Parmesan and a beaten egg. If the mixture is too soft add a little breadcrumbs.
4. Mix everything and form some slightly crushed sausages.
5. Pass them in the flour then in the egg and finally in the breadcrumbs mixed with corn flour.
6. Sauté them again in the egg and again in the bread and corn in order to create a crisp and homogeneous breading.
7. Heat two tablespoons of oil in a pan and cook the sticks by turning them for a few minutes until the breading is golden brown.

Tips: You can also prepare them fried or baked and use other types of vegetables according to your tastes.

PREPARATION: 20 M **DIFFICULTY: LOW** **COOKING TIME: 15 M**

HAZELNUT SPREADABLE CREAM (HOMEMADE NUTELLA) – DESSERT

INGREDIENTS

- 4 oz. of milk chocolate
- 4 oz. of toasted hazelnuts
- 4 oz. of icing sugar
- 4 oz. of butter
- 1 sachet of vanillin

DIRECTIONS

1. Melt the chocolate with the butter
2. Blend the hazelnuts very finely together with the sugar and vanillin so that the hazelnuts do not release too much oil and put them in the saucepan together with the other ingredients.
3. Cook for 10 minutes on very low heat (preferably in a bain-marie) must not boil. If necessary, add a little milk. Stir constantly until you get a thick cream.
4. Pour it into the sterilized jars, cap them and turn them upside down.
5. Let cool to room temperature.

Tips: keep it closed at room temperature while when you open it, it is better to keep it in the fridge. It will tend to harden but keeping it a few minutes out of the fridge and mixing it with a teaspoon will return it soft.

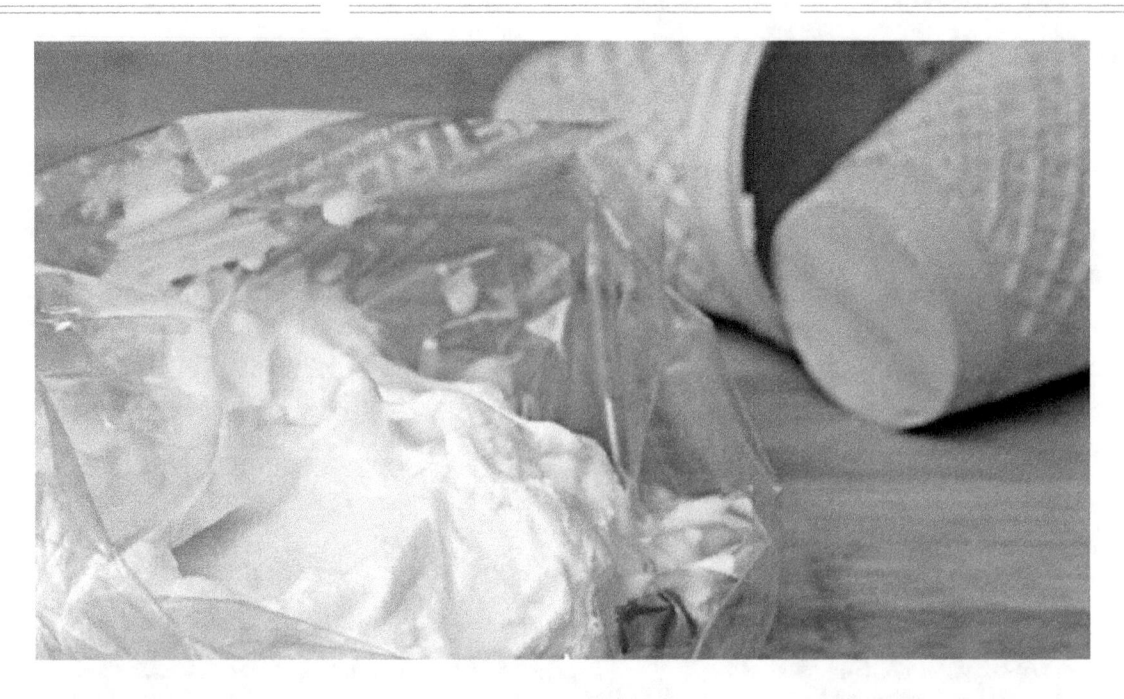

PREPARATION: 20 M **DIFFICULTY: LOW** **COOKING TIME: 0 M**

ICE CREAM IN A BAG - DESSERT

INGREDIENTS

- 1 cup of fresh liquid cream
- 4 oz. of condensed milk
- 2 oz. of icing sugar
- Additional tools:
- 1 small freeze bag
- 1 large freeze bag
- Ice cubes
- 5 tbsp. coarse salt
- 1 clothespin

DIRECTIONS

1. Take the condensed milk and put it in a bowl together with the fresh liquid cream and icing sugar. Mix well with a spoon to even out the ingredients.
2. Put all the mixture in a freezing bag and close it well with a tight knot.
3. Also, put a clothespin to hang over the knot so that you are sure that nothing will come out anyway.
4. Put the small bag inside the large bag with lots of ice cubes and coarse salt.
5. Close the big bag with a tight knot. Well, the method to do this is to beat the bag quickly so that the mixture is well beaten inside, the ice together with the salt will melt more slowly so when the ice cream is melted it will be ready.
6. It will take about 20 minutes, when you will open the bag the ice cream was ready!

Tips: another much more fun method is to start playing by throwing the bag with each other. The more you throw it and the beat it, obviously the better your ice cream will be. You can also use vegetable cream. Of course, you can also make it classically by putting it in the ice-cream maker

PREPARATION: 15 M   **DIFFICULTY: LOW**   **COOKING TIME: 0 M**

WAFER ICE CREAM CAKE - DESSERT

INGREDIENTS

- 2 lb. of cream ice cream (if you want to prepare it at home you can follow the recipe Ice cream in a bag)
- 9 oz. of cocoa wafers
- 7 oz. of chocolate spreadable cream (if you want to prepare it at home you can follow the recipe Hazelnut spreadable cream - Homemade Nutella)
- 5 tbsp. of fresh liquid cream

For the topping:
- Chocolate spreadable cream
- Chopped hazelnuts

DIRECTIONS

1. Take a baking pan possibly with an openable hinge and line it with cling film.
2. Cut the wafers into 3 parts each to create many small squares and place them all on the base of the cake pan as close as possible.
3. Mix the chocolate cream in a bowl with the fresh cream (not whipped) in order to make it more fluid and pour it on the wafers in the cake pan to fill all the spaces.
4. Put the pan in the freezer for a few minutes.
5. Take the creamy ice-cream and mix it well with a spoon so that it becomes creamy and pour it over the chocolate cream which will have started to harden.
6. Level the surface well then take the chocolate cream with a spoon and pour it over the surface of the cake. It does not need to be precise.
7. Finish by sprinkling the whole croissant cake with the chopped peanuts and put in the freezer for 30 minutes.

Tips: take the cake out of the freezer 15 minutes before serving. You can create the base with mixed dark chocolate and fresh cream. Do not make the wafer ice cream cake only with melted dark chocolate otherwise, you will not be able to cut it once frozen.

PREPARATION: 15 M **DIFFICULTY: LOW** **COOKING TIME: 10 M**

NUTELLA BISCUIT - BREAKFAST

INGREDIENTS

- 5 oz. of flour
- 2 eggs
- 3 oz. sugar
- 2½ oz. butter
- 3 tbsp. of milk
- 1 oz. of cocoa powder
- 1/2 sachet of yeast
- 1 pinch of salt
- Nutella (if you want to prepare it at home you can follow the recipe Hazelnut spreadable cream - Homemade Nutella)

DIRECTIONS

1. Put the flour, baking powder, sugar, cocoa powder, salt, eggs, milk and butter at room temperature in a bowl and mix well until you get homogeneous dough.
2. Roll the dough into two sheets of parchment paper until it is about half a cm thick.
3. Cut with a pastry cutter or with a glass many round parts.
4. In half the rounds that you have created, put a teaspoon of Nutella and cover with the remaining rounds, sealing the edges well so that it does not come out during cooking.
5. Put your biscuit on a pan with parchment paper and cook them in a preheated oven at 180° for about 10 minutes.

Tips: do not prolong the cooking times too much, otherwise you will risk drying the Nutella inside.

PREPARATION: 15 M **DIFFICULTY: MEDIUM** **COOKING TIME: 10 M**

BULL'S EYE BISCUITS - BREAKFAST

INGREDIENTS

- 2 cup of Flour
- 2 Stick of Butter
- 4 oz. of sugar
- 1 yolk
- Jam of your favorite taste
- Icing sugar

DIRECTIONS

1. 1.Put the butter at room temperature in a bowl and add the sugar.
2. 2. Turn with a spoonful of butter and sugar so that they become a cream.
3. 3. Add the egg yolk and let it be absorbed by butter and sugar.
4. 4. Gradually add all the flour, mixing with a spoon and then kneading with your hands until a homogeneous mixture is obtained.
5. 5. Roll out the shortcrust pastry between two sheets of parchment paper with a rolling pin.
6. 6. Cut all the pastry with a pastry cutter or with a round shape from biscuits then in the middle of the biscuits there are also make a hole in the center.
7. 7. Bake all the cookies with and without a hole in a preheated oven ventilated at 180° for about 10 minutes.
8. 8. Remove from the oven and let them cool completely.
9. 9. Sprinkle all the biscuits with the hole with icing sugar while those without the hole spread them with jam and cover them with the biscuits with the hole.

Tips: you can stuff the bull's eye with anything you want. You can add a sachet of vanillin to the pastry dough.

PREPARATION: 15 M **DIFFICULTY: LOW** **COOKING TIME: 25 M**

VEGETABLE (MEAT)BALLS - MAIN COURSE

INGREDIENTS

- 3 courgettes
- 2 carrots
- 3 tablespoons of grated Parmesan
- 1 spoon bread crumbs
- 1 egg

DIRECTIONS

1. Clean and cut the carrots and courgettes and boil them.
2. Drain them, squeeze them very well and blend them together with the egg.
3. Add 3 tablespoons of grated Parmesan and 1 tablespoon of breadcrumbs to the mixture.
4. Mix everything well and, with the help of a spoon, form slightly crushed meatballs that you will cook in a baking tin.
5. Bake them with parchment paper lightly greased with oil at 200° for about 25 minutes until they turn golden brown.

Tips: if you want to prepare zucchini and carrot balls, you can also combine a boiled potato with the dough. If the dough is too soft you can add a spoonful of breadcrumbs again. I prefer not to add salt because the Parmesan is already present which is quite tasty but if you want you can add a pinch in the dough before forming the meatballs.

PREPARATION: 10 M **DIFFICULTY: MEDIUM** **COOKING TIME: 50 M**

ACCORDION POTATOES - MAIN COURSE

INGREDIENTS

- 4 medium potatoes
- 1½ oz. of Parmesan cheese
- 1½ oz. of butter
- Salt

DIRECTIONS

1. Take the potatoes, peel them and rinse them under running tap water then dry them well.
2. Make many cuts on the potatoes but do not cut them completely, only halfway leaving the bottom part intact.
3. Put all the potatoes engraved on a baking sheet with parchment paper and salt them lightly.
4. Put the potatoes in a preheated oven at 180° for 40 minutes until they are practically cooked.
5. Remove the potatoes from the oven and put a little parmesan cheese on top of each trying to go into the cuts and a few flakes of butter.
6. Put the potatoes back in the oven raising it up to 200° and let them cook for about 10 minutes.
7. Remove the accordion potatoes from the oven and serve hot, warm or even cold.

Tips: if you want you can also put slices of cheese between the cuts of the potatoes, obviously the last 10 minutes only. You can put chopped aromatic herbs on the potatoes. Remove the accordion potatoes from the oven only when they have created a golden crust on the surface.

PREPARATION: 20 M **DIFFICULTY: MEDIUM** **COOKING TIME: 20 M**

FISH-BALLS - MAIN COURSE

INGREDIENTS

- 12 oz. of salmon fillet
- 3 oz. of Parmesan cheese
- 3 oz. of Bread
- 1 egg
- Parsley
- Milk
- Bread crumbs
- Extra virgin olive oil
- Salt

DIRECTIONS

1. Heat the milk slightly and soak the chopped bread.
2. Cook the salmon (if you have no other leftover fish) in a non-stick pan for 10/15 minutes until well cooked.
3. Finely chop the parsley.
4. Squeeze the bread out of the milk and put it in a bowl.
5. Crumble the cooked salmon and put it in the bowl with the soaked bread.
6. Add a pinch of salt, the whole egg and the chopped parsley and mix everything well.
7. Form the meatballs with your hands and pass them in the breadcrumbs.
8. Put all the salmon balls on a baking tin with parchment paper and sprinkle them lightly with extra virgin olive oil.
9. Cook the fish-balls in a preheated oven at 180° for about 25 minutes, turning them halfway through cooking.

Tips: you can replace the bread soaked in milk with 80 grams of ricotta cheese. If you want you can add half a clove of minced garlic to the meatball mixture. You can also use other types of advanced fish.

PREPARATION: 10 M **DIFFICULTY: LOW** **COOKING TIME: 15 M**

BAKED POTATO CHIPS - SNACK

INGREDIENTS

- 2 medium-small potatoes
- Extra virgin olive oil
- Salt

DIRECTIONS

1. Wash the potatoes very well with the peel and dry them.
2. Cut many possibly thin slices (if you have the mandolin it is even better) and put them on a sheet of parchment paper on a pan.
3. Salt and sprinkle the surface with extra virgin olive oil.
4. Put in a preheated oven at 200° for about 15 minutes, turning them on the other side halfway through cooking.

Tips: if you want you can sprinkle on the potatoes also chili, oregano or grated parmesan cheese and they will become even tastier

PREPARATION: 5 M   **DIFFICULTY: LOW**   **COOKING TIME: 10 M**

PARMESAN LOLLIPOP - SNACK

INGREDIENTS

- Parmesan (better not to use the already grated Parmesan)
- Sesame
- Wooden sticks from skewers

DIRECTIONS

1. Grate the Parmesan
2. Mix it with a little bit of toasted sesame seeds. If you do not find them on the market already toasted, just put them two or three minutes in the oven.
3. Create small piles with the parmesan and sesame mixture on a sheet of parchment paper. If you have a pastry cutter help yourself with that otherwise do like me that I used a cup.
4. When you have created the pile, crush it a little with your hands and flatten it.
5. Cut the skewer sticks into two and place one on each pile.
6. Cover the end of the toothpick with a little grated Parmesan and bake for about 10 minutes.
7. Remove from the oven and let cool well before pulling them up.

Tips: as soon as they are baked they will still be soft, you have to wait until they cool completely to remove them from the parchment paper. If you want you can also prepare them in a pan over very low heat.

PREPARATION: 15 M   **DIFFICULTY: LOW**   **COOKING TIME: 15 M**

STUFFED BREADSTICKS - SNACK

INGREDIENTS

- 2 rolls of puff pastry
- 4 oz. of cold cuts (you can choose any type of cold cuts to make the stuffed breadsticks)
- 2 oz. of Parmesan cheese
- 1 egg
- Milk

DIRECTIONS

1. Unroll the two rolls of rectangular puff pastry and brush one with the beaten egg white.
2. Chop the cold cut you have chosen in the mixer or with the crescent or knife and distribute it completely over the puff pastry brushed with egg white evenly.
3. Sprinkle all the puff pastry with grated Parmesan.
4. Put the second roll of puff pastry on top of the first and press well with your hands and roll them out with a rolling pin so as to thin them well.
5. Cut many strips with a very sharp knife in the short sense of the puff pastry and then roll them with your hands.
6. Put all the stuffed breadsticks on a pan with parchment paper and brush them either with milk or even with the egg yolk.
7. Bake the stuffed breadsticks in a preheated oven at 180° for about 15 minutes until the puff pastry is cooked and golden brown.

Tips: you can also make them only with cheeses if you have vegetarian friends. You can replace the parmesan with Pecorino. They are delicious both hot and cold.

PREPARATION: 10 M   **DIFFICULTY: LOW**   **COOKING TIME: 20 M**

STUFFED APPLES - DESSERT

INGREDIENTS

- 4 apples
- ½ cup of fresh cream
- 2 oz. raisins
- Half glass of water
- 4 tablespoons of honey

DIRECTIONS

1. Soak the raisins in water.
2. Wash the apples thoroughly and cut the upper cap with a knife.
3. Remove the core and empty the apple with the help of a spoon leaving a finger around the perimeter in this way.
4. Put the apple pulp in a bowl and cut it into small pieces where you will combine the cream, honey, and the drained and squeezed raisins.
5. Mix well with a spoon and fill each apple with the mixture obtained.
6. Pour a little stuffing over the caps too and bake in a preheated oven at 180° for about 20 minutes.
7. Take out of the oven and serve hot or lukewarm.

Tips: you can also add macaroons or biscuits crumbled to the filling and give a crunchy note. If you want you can cook them in the microwave for obviously less (more or less 6 minutes) at 700 watts. Council not to empty the apple too much but to leave a layer of at least half a cm otherwise in cooking they will risk to collapse too much as it happened to me instead the beauty is that they remain whole.

PREPARATION: 30 M **DIFFICULTY: MEDIUM** **COOKING TIME: 40 M**

HOMEMADE KINDER PARADISO - DESSERT

INGREDIENTS

- Ingredients for the cake:
- 4½ oz. of flour
- 4½ oz. of granulated sugar
- 1 oz. of corn starch
- Zest of 1 lemon
- 2 whole eggs and 2 yolks (room temperature)
- 1½ oz. grams of butter
- 1 pinch of salt
- ½ sachet vanilla yeast for desserts
- Half vial of vanilla flavor

- Ingredients for the cream:
- 2 cup of whole milk (preferably fresh)
- 1 cup of fresh

DIRECTIONS

1. Whip the 2 whole eggs and two yolks (keep the two egg whites aside) together with the sugar until they become a white and frothy mixture.
2. Add the lemon zest and half a vial of vanilla flavoring.
3. Put the mixed flour, starch, salt and yeast in a bowl and start adding them to the egg mixture, mixing gently with a spatula.
4. Beat the two remaining egg whites until stiff and incorporate them into the rest of the dough.
5. Now add the melted but COLD butter and mix well.
6. Grease a mold (rectangular is better... I used the 30 × 20 disposable aluminum ones) and pour the mixture.
7. Bake in a hot oven at 180° for about 30 minutes. Turn off the oven and leave the cake in the oven again for 10 minutes while you prepare the cream.
8. Heat the milk with the other half a vial of vanilla flavor.
9. Put the cornstarch and sugar in a bowl and slowly pour the hot milk mixing with a whisk. Put on the heat and cook until it boils, thicken a few minutes and let cool to room temperature then cover with plastic wrap (otherwise the skin will form on top) and let cool in the fridge.
10. Whip the cream and add it to the rest of the cooled cream, mixing from bottom to top.
11. Also, add the honey and mix everything.

INGREDIENTS

cream
- 3 teaspoons of honey
- Half vial of vanilla flavor
- 2 oz. of corn starch
- 4 oz. of granulated sugar
- Icing sugar to taste

DIRECTIONS

12. Cut the cake in half horizontally and fill it with plenty of milk cream. Cover with the other half of the cake and sprinkle with icing sugar.

Tips: cut the slices only at the last moment and cold in the fridge in order to facilitate the operation. If you prefer to make a round cake, I recommend a 10 inches mold

BASIC NUTRITION AND WHY IT'S IMPORTANT
(CHAPTER FOR PARENTS)

Healthy eating

Nutrition is one of the most determining behaviors in the health of children, as well as in that of adults. If children take on incorrect eating habits, they will probably continue when they grow up, but if they understand their importance from an early age, it will be easier for them to take care of them as adults. To teach children what it means to eat healthily, you can adopt some strategies that stimulate their curiosity by avoiding boring them with difficult words. Children like to know the why of things, as they struggle to accept behavior for which they cannot find an explanation. Then tell them what nutrients make them strong like superheroes and beautiful like princes, using their favorite fantasy characters as examples. Use this card for less appreciated foods and take advantage of it to explain its nutritional value.

For example, if children struggle to accept fish, tell them that it is thanks to this food that pirates are so smart because it contains precious fats that have the name of a secret ingredient, omega 3, which are good for the brain and make those who eat them smarter. If the kids object to you, the kind that Peter Pan defeated the pirates, you tell them it was only because he ate more fish than Captain Hook. If your children ask you for a snack instead of the apple you are offering, reveal that Rapunzel has managed to make her hair strong enough to escape the tower thanks to the apples, which are good for hair and skin because they contain many vitamins, like all fruit. Through children's fairy tales and favorite stories, you can explain the nutritional content of food to them in a fun way. Also, if the children refuse a food, do not be discouraged: you can try again after a few weeks, perhaps cooking them differently.

What Are the Nutrients?

Explaining what nutrients are to children is a demanding task, but discovering the role of healthy nutrition and the function of food could become a game or a fairy tale to tell. You can start with the distinction between foods and nutrients, illustrating the substances contained in the food that allow you to carry out all the activities, from play to study, taking as an example a typical family lunch and demonstrating how this meal provides a very large amount of nutrients.

Making such a complex and delicate topic less boring will help you improve the idea that children have healthy foods, such as fruit and vegetables. By explaining the history of nutrients and their role within the body, you will have the opportunity to make them more captivating and to respond to your children's curiosity. In fact, they will wonder why mom and dad insist on the importance of all kinds of green leaves, or fish, which has so many unpleasant bones: it will be your opportunity to tell how many good things these foods can do, thanks to the substances that contain. If children tend to avoid certain foods, it's time to tell something more than the usual health story: you can give them a good motivation for each food, explaining what proteins, carbohydrates, vitamins, salts are for minerals and fats.

After talking to the children about the miraculous properties of nutrients, it's time to present them at the table: then you can make the food more appetizing and interesting in the eyes of a child and invite him to prepare the dishes together with you, so that he learns to recognize the foods and their transformation when served at the table. You can invent exploratory food routes that illustrate nutrients from time to time, so that children begin to associate nutritional properties and their functions with certain foods. Every day, you can take a moment to illustrate a nutrient, inviting the children to the kitchen to discover fruit, vegetables, meat or fish, to then cook and offer them at the table.

In this way, you can also build a weekly diet that includes the ideal portions of the food and from time to time tell the children something while you are in the kitchen. While they are fascinated by your cooking skills, surprise them with the irresistible stories of the benefits that nutrients bring to the body daily. Carbohydrates, proteins, minerals, vitamins and fats will turn into the daily heroes of children.

Carbohydrates

Start talking to children about the nutrients and carbohydrates are the ideal substances, because the foods that contain them are among the most loved ones. It will be important to tell them what carbohydrates do in our body and which is the best food, also trying to offer the healthiest foods and explain to children that sweets are not prohibited but should be eaten in moderation. Start by saying that carbohydrates are the fuel of the human body, that is, they provide the fundamental energy for every action that children perform. Carbohydrates, however, are not all the same: there are simple ones, sugars, which turn into energy to be used quickly, and complex ones, or starch, which instead offers energy to be consumed more slowly.

At this point, try to imagine carbohydrates together with your children: imagine a great forge, in which these nutrients work to provide for the vigor of children. The action of carbohydrates is a bit like that of a fireplace, which must always be powered to keep the fire lit: explain to the children that to feed energy, which is the body's fire, a healthy diet needs the carbohydrates. These nutrients work to make children feel strong and active: sugars help them with the activities they carry out immediately, for example when they have to face a workout or a game, or even when they have fun running in the open air, while carbohydrates complex are the sustenance that keeps their body in force daily and constantly. You just have to reveal to children where these miraculous substances are contained: surprise them by explaining that simple carbohydrates are not only found in sugar and sweets, but also in honey, jams, and fruit. Then tell us where they can find complex carbohydrates, which will always support them in the most important meals to face the day, such as breakfast and lunch: in fact, the bread, rusks and cereals eaten for breakfast are rich in starch, as well as the pasta, rice, and potatoes, which are often the main course of lunch.

Proteins

There are other nutrients well known for being essential to the proper functioning of the body: proteins, which are the most common component in the body after water. These substances are the best friends of growth because their job is to manufacture and renew all the tissues that make up the body. Even proteins are not all the same, there are animal and vegetable proteins: the former contains all the essential amino acids, while to have a similar supply of amino acids from vegetables, you need to eat several types. Then the children will ask you: what are amino acids? They are like rings that join together in a circle to form proteins, which are the building blocks of the body. In this way, the human body begins to resemble a very complicated and fascinating construction, in which each piece has its role.

Proteins are truly exceptional substances: as a highly efficient team, they divide the tasks, completing various commitments. Some come together as bricks to create the tissues, others have long legs to carry many substances in the blood that cannot move on their own, still, others intervene instead to help the immune system and the metabolism, or contribute to form other components that regulate the mood and sleep of young and old. Let the children imagine proteins as the body's superheroes, who work hard to make everything work better, because they care about the health of the body and mind. To make the story more fun, you can free your children's imagination by inviting them to draw how these substances are imagined. Finally, show them the exquisite foods in which proteins are contained. Since those of animal origin must be eaten no more than a few times a week, from time to time remind them that a tasty egg in the eye or the chicken breast with lemon that you are preparing helps to stack those precious bricks. And remind them that even when you prepare many types of vegetables or legumes, it is to provide them with the best amount of protein, as well as other basic nutrients.

The fats

Even fats, despite their bad reputation, are very important nutrients for children: they are the ones that, together with carbohydrates, give energy and represent an unlimited reserve to face physical activity. But fats also have other fundamental functions: they contribute to cellular metabolism and carry some vitamins, precious for the health of children. One thing your kids don't know about fats is that they form exceptional relays along with other substances. For example, they are precursors to some regulators of different systems in the body: this means that fats initiate certain activities of the immune system, the cardiovascular system, and renal function. But this is not the only reason why they are so important for children: fats are also good for the nervous system, promoting the capacity to focus, attention, and activities such as reading and writing. Some fats in particular—omega 3—are fantastic for helping children in school.

Omega 3 is even essential for the body because it can only be taken with food. In addition, these fats help against inflammation, as well as promoting cognitive growth and development. That's why it is important to take the fats in the right quantities, without exaggerating, and through the healthiest and most nutritious foods. Perhaps it will be difficult to explain to children that fats are not only contained in sweets—which are high in sugars, but you can teach them to appreciate all the foods that contain them.

A very beneficial fat, for example, is extra virgin olive oil, which is so good that even a simple salad is tasty. Even butter, eaten fresh and in small doses, is a good fat, which you can add to the rusks with jam, for a delicious breakfast. Fats are also contained in many protein foods, such as milk, which is also essential for starting the day of the little ones.

Vitamins

A micronutrient that you hear so much about are vitamins, useful in promoting the proper functioning of the body. Vitamins must be taken by eating and are mainly present in fruits and vegetables, which thanks to them have the reputation of being among the healthiest and most important foods of all ages.

Vitamins have the names of the letters of the alphabet: to tell what they are used for, you can make children draw colored letters, also adding nice faces. You can also draw the letters of vitamins with fruit when you prepare a snack for the little ones. Being able to remember all the functions of the different vitamins is difficult even for adults, so it will be difficult for children too, but they can have fun drawing and coloring them, while you will explain to them from time to time that the dishes you prepare contain a handful of vitamins, so you will have the opportunity to talk about their benefits. The most important vitamins for children are A, C, and D, but also those of group B, because they contribute to the growth and well-being of the organism, being beneficial for the eyesight, for the development of the bones, for the system immune and cell renewal. To make the vitamins more fun, combine them with the colors of fruit and vegetables.

For example, vitamin A is present in milk and eggs but also in red, yellow and orange vegetables, such as carrots, apricots, tomatoes and berries. Vitamin C is good with the orange and green colors, in fact you find it especially in citrus fruits, spinach, broccoli and kiwis: when the cold season threatens you with influences and colds, you have to rely on this substance.

Mineral salts

Mineral salts, like vitamins, do not provide energy but are very important for the body, and their deficiency is to be avoided especially in the evolutionary phase. It is not difficult to assimilate them, because they are present in almost all foods, but some get along well with particular substances rather than others. For example, tell your children how happy the marriage between iron and vitamin C is: together, these two substances are invincible, the vitamin supports the mineral, and they are a real cure-all for the body.

Among the most important minerals during growth are iron and calcium: an iron deficiency, in fact, can lead to anemia, while the lack of calcium is dangerous for the bones. This is why it is necessary to promote the absorption of minerals by eating in a healthy and balanced way. For proper iron intake, children need to eat meat, cereals, green leafy vegetables, such as spinach, and legumes. Since the meat is placed in a higher position in the food pyramid, try to favor vegetables and legumes, telling your children how they make them strong. Calcium, on the other hand, is present mainly in milk and its derivatives, which for this reason are fundamental in childhood. The best time to absorb calcium is for breakfast or a snack, when you can indulge your children with a cup of milk or yogurt.

Other mineral salts are also important for the health of children: for example, phosphorus, potassium, and magnesium, which are a cure-all for the psychophysical well-being of children. When you offer fruit, especially bananas, apricots, and citrus fruits, tell the children that they will have a feast of potassium, while when you serve cereals, peas and beans on the table, remind them how important magnesium is. If the little ones don't like fish, tell them how important phosphorus is for memory: this, together with omega 3s, helps to learn and is therefore the secret ingredient for doing well in school.

Finally, another nice way and creative to explain all there is to know about nutrients could be the coloring food pyramid, which you could print and color your children: the pyramid will have a color for daily food, one for weekly food and another for those who eat every now and then.

Printed in the USA
CPSIA information can be obtained
at www.ICGtesting.com
LVHW062332011224
798082LV00013B/1242